BIG FISH FROM SMALL WATERS

ALSO BY KENNETH SEAMAN
Canal Fishing

BIG FISH
FROM SMALL
WATERS

By

KENNETH SEAMAN

Line Illustrations by Ernest Petts

DAVID & CHARLES : NEWTON ABBOT

ISBN 0 7153 5937 1

Set in 11 on 13 point Garamond
and printed in Great Britain
by Latimer Trend & Company Ltd Plymouth
for David & Charles (Holdings) Limited
South Devon House   Newton Abbot   Devon

Contents

Illustrations

Illustrations

I

The Nature of
Small Waters

DIFFERENT STREAMS AND THEIR FISH

STREAMS and small rivers are probably the most numerous and yet the most underfished of all waters. Only a few of the best and most carefully tended are fished intensively. Some rarely, if ever, see an angler on their banks—possibly because they are so small, insignificant, and overgrown that many anglers think they are unfishable. Yet most of these streams will contain fish, and some fish of specimen size. I have seen a 3lb trout caught from a tiny rivulet only a foot across, and have caught roach over 2lb, and chub over 5lb, from streams which one could span with outstretched legs.

At first it might seem difficult to judge what species of fish a stream is likely to contain, but once the angler has learned to recognise the obvious signs he can often assess quite accurately just how rich in fish life each stream is likely to be. In general, the best of these small waters are clear, and rich in plant and animal life. The poorest are rocky and almost totally devoid of either plant or animal life. These differences are inevitably reflected in the number and size of the fish to be found in each water. In the world of nature everything is interdependent: a water that is rich in natural organic foods often contains large fish of several different species, whereas a water of poor quality will rarely contain big fish. By comparison, the size of the water itself is unimportant. The smallest of streams may contain many fine fish, while larger rivers and streams may hold few, if any.

The Mountain Stream

It is not by accident that the poorest streams are found most frequently in mountain regions, where the temperature is generally low, the water fast-moving, and the bed of the stream too hard and rocky to support an abundant growth of weed. In consequence, these streams are usually deficient in plant, animal, and fish life. Small trout are often the only occupants, and are almost entirely dependent upon the meagre quantities of flies and their larvae that are indigenous to these mountain regions. In some streams the trout develop cannibal tendencies, and thus become self-limiting. Very rarely are any significant numbers of coarse fish found, although in some streams the trout may share its domain with bullheads and crayfish. Because living space is restricted and the competition for food intense, the trout remain stunted, and are comparatively easy to catch.

In their lower reaches these mountain streams gradually acquire a different character. The current slackens its pace, the stream becomes wider, the deep holding pools more numerous, and the weed-growth more abundant. Under these conditions the fish population gradually becomes more abundant and more varied—although, in Ireland, Wales, and Scotland, where coarse fish are less numerous, the trout usually remain the dominant species. In England, such fish as roach, dace, and chub begin to appear in increasing numbers; and finally, in the deeper, slower-moving, lowland reaches of the stream, perch, bream, and pike may also be found. Each stream is different; each has its own individual character; each its own variety of fish.

The Lowland Stream

Streams which have their source in the lowlands are usually vastly different in character from the mountain streams. They are often wider and slower-moving, and contain a more abundant growth of weed and a much greater variety of fish. Only in the most jealously preserved streams will the trout remain the dominant species; elsewhere, it will share its domain with numerous coarse fish. Small fish, such as loach, bullheads, gudgeon, minnows, and sticklebacks—all of which are an essential part of the food chain—are plentiful in most lowland streams, where animal life is also much more abundant. The faster parts of the stream usually contain, in season, many nymphs, together with leeches and caddis grubs, while the slower-moving stretches will harbour colonies of freshwater shrimps and chironomid larvae, together with an assortment of beetles, pondskaters, and nymphs.

Weeds of both the submerged and the emergent variety are also found in much greater quantity and density in lowland streams; and in the pellucid waters of chalk streams may grow so lushly that frequent cutting is necessary to keep them in check. As a result of this lush growth of weed and abundance of animal life, the fish are usually of much greater size than those to be found in mountain streams.

The Overgrown Stream

Some streams wind slowly across flat meadow lands, their banks totally devoid of vegetation, apart from an occasional leaning ash, willow, or alder tree. Others are densely overgrown; in some cases so much so that at first sight it seems impossible to fish them with rod and line. Bushes and trees encroach thickly over the water. Dense masses of weeds, some of which might be as tall as a grown man, form an almost impenetrable barrier along the banks of the stream. But good fish can be caught from these overgrown streams if the angler will regard the difficulties they present as a challenge, rather than an insurmountable obstacle. Over many years of fishing this type of stream I have not yet encountered one from which it was impossible to catch fish.

In many of these streams even the water itself is densely overgrown, the weed in some swims stretching from bank to bank in a solid mass. In other swims tangled masses of debris, composed of fallen branches and other rubbish, form dense barriers across the stream. Such places seem intimidating, but the thoughtful angler will realise that they not only provide hiding-places for the fish, but for himself, too.

LIGHT EFFECTS ON CLEAR STREAMS

In some streams the water is of such perfect clarity that the fish can often be seen, hanging in the current as if preserved in glass. When the sun is on the water everything—fish, weeds, and even the stones on the bottom—are sharply and clearly illumined. Fish, under these conditions, are usually more wary than usual, more susceptible to carelessly-cast shadows, and consequently more difficult to catch.

When the water is low and the sun bright, they will tend to retreat under weeds and undercut banks, or into the deepest recesses of the pools; and, in summer, up into the fast, broken water where they can lie unseen. Trout, especially, love this fast water, but chub, dace, roach, and even perch, can often be found there, too, during the early part of the season when the minnows are congregated on the shallows. Fish respond quickly to changes in the height, colour, and temperature of the water; and in the summer they find in the fast currents, oxygen and many of the food organisms upon which they feed. Remembering this will help the angler to decide where fish are most likely to be at any given time.

THE EFFECT OF SPATE CONDITIONS

After a period of heavy rain a rapid change occurs in both the height and the colour of the water. Mountain streams rise rapidly and fall rapidly, and though the spate may be heavy, it is usually of short duration. In contrast, the slower-moving, deeper streams of the lowlands rise more slowly, but maintain the new height and colour of the water for much longer.

The spate has a marked effect on the fish in the stream. No longer will they be found mainly in the fast, oxygenated water, or in hiding-places beneath weeds and other debris. Instead, they will tend to move slowly into the slacker areas of water at the edges of the fast currents, and into those places which, during the low-water period, were extremely shallow. Cattle-drinks, bends in the stream, and the mouths of tiny feeder streams become

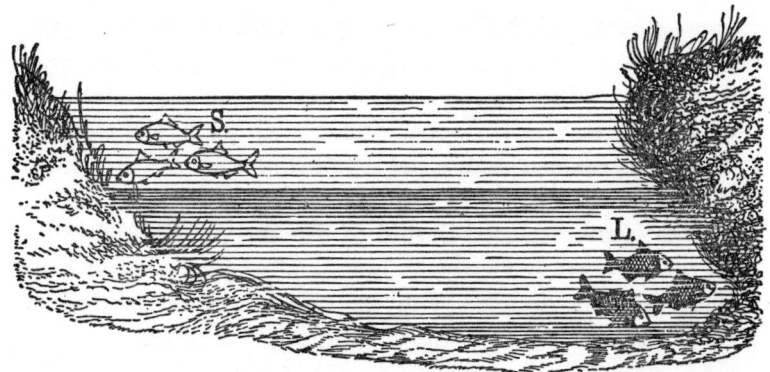

Fig 1   *Cross-section of stream showing how the current has created an undercut bank on the deeper side. 'L' indicates where the fish are most likely to be when the water is at normal or low level; 'S' where they are most likely to be when the stream is in spate*

much-favoured places in which fish of many different species can be found (Fig 1).

During periods of extreme spate, when the water spills over into the surrounding fields, fish can sometimes be caught there, too, whereas the very fast water, now become a roaring torrent, will hold comparatively few fish. Only trout, sea-trout, and salmon seem to enjoy this new, strong flush of water which stimulates them out of their low-water lethargy and sends them forging on upstream once more.

While the spate is at its height most fish eat very little, but as soon as it begins to subside and the water starts to clear, they often feed eagerly, and this can be one of the best times for the angler to seek all species of fish. Even the clearest of streams usually fishes well after a spate.

LOW TEMPERATURE EFFECTS

Seasonal changes in temperature also affect both the stream and its fish. In autumn, when the leaves begin to fall and the weeds to die off, the water often acquires a glass-like clarity, and the fish become more difficult to catch. At this time of the year it is possible to walk carefully up the banks of some streams without seeing a single fish. It might even seem that there are no fish in the stream. But, in fact, the fish are still there, in the deepest water and under the banks where the sun's rays cannot reach them. and the keen eyes of their enemies cannot perceive them.

At dusk, when the light begins to fade, swims which only a few hours earlier seemed devoid of fish become suddenly alive with them. There is a tell-tale 'humping' of the water, and the surface becomes dimpled with rings as fish begin to feed off floating insects, or flies that have fallen into the water.

At this time of the year fish do not feed as freely during the daytime as they did during the warm summer months. When the water is low, dusk is often the best time to seek them. Only during a spate, and while the water still retains some colour, can the angler expect to catch many fish during the day. Low autumn temperatures, combined with low, clear water, will make it extremely difficult to catch most species of fish at all.

THE STREAM IN WINTER

When winter proper arrives, and most of the fallen leaves have been swept away by successive spates, the fishing in many streams gradually improves again. The fish, by now accustomed to the change in the temperature of the water, often feed more freely than they did during the low-water period of autumn. The deeper pools, and the slower-moving swims edged by decaying masses of reeds, are often the best places to fish. The shallow, fast-moving water will contain very few coarse fish during the daylight hours.

From Christmas on until the end of the coarse-fishing season in March, the angler can usually expect to reap his richest rewards from the small streams. The weather is milder, and the bed of the stream will have been swept clean of debris by many roaring spates. The fish, too, are often at their best: fat-bodied, strong, and brilliant of fin and eye. Some of the best catches, and some of the largest individual fish I have ever caught from streams, have been taken during this period.

2

Angling in Streams

THE ANGLER'S APPROACH

MY ANGLING apprenticeship was served on the banks of a stream, hunting the sticklebacks that could often be seen moving in vast shoals above the billowing masses of submerged weed; and if I could start all over again I would not change this. Small stream are great teachers. The angler who wishes to understand fish, to observe them at close quarters, and to learn how to catch them, cannot do better than start by angling in these small, overgrown waters. The larger rivers may offer greater scope, more room to fish, and larger catches of fish; but in none of them will the angler ever find the same opportunity to observe and catch fish at close quarters that he will find in the small streams.

To catch any fish can be an exciting and rewarding experience; but that experience becomes more satisfying and more meaningful if the angler has a sound knowledge of the fish and its habits. The angler who fishes without this knowledge can still catch some fish. He might, with luck, sometimes catch a lot of them; but his fishing will lack direction and understanding, and some measure of enjoyment. By contrast, the angler who has his finger on the pulse of the river will learn to understand its many different moods, and much that is valuable about its fish. He will learn when his chances are highest, and when they are lowest; where to seek each species in many different conditions of water and weather; and what baits they are most likely to take. His fishing will not be based on the flimsy foundations of luck and chance, but rather on a sound knowledge of the water and its fish, built up over many years of fishing and observing. And no water is so well suited to the acquisition of this essential knowledge than the small, clear stream.

The overgrown nature of many of the swims permits him to get close to the fish without being seen himself. The relative smallness of the swims also means that, no matter where he casts his bait, it will seldom be far away from a fish. The fish is therefore more likely to see the bait and, provided it has not been scared, is also more likely to take it. Something like 90 per cent of all the fish I have caught from streams have been caught at less than 10yd range, and many of them by fishing virtually under the rod-tip.

Any angler who wishes to succeed in these small waters must also learn to be versatile. Each swim is different in some way; each poses its own special, individual problems. Some swims consist only of tiny pools, fringed by tall reeds or bushes. Others are densely overgrown with thickets of willow or alder. Some are shallow and swift-moving. Others are deep and slow-moving. No swim should be overlooked, no matter how small, how insignificant, or how overgrown it may appear. Quite often, the largest fish will be found in the most unlikely swim.

Concealment

Concealment is another aspect of stream fishing which the angler should study. Beds of tall reeds or grasses should never be beaten down as they provide natural hiding-places. Bushes, trees and weeds, even bends in the stream, can all be utilised in the same way. Where there is no cover at all it is always advisable to fish upstream rather than down. The angler who places himself upstream of the fish merely because it seems easier to fish downstream, prejudices his chances considerably. Comfort or convenience should never be allowed to take precedence over the more important matter of remaining concealed. The successful stream angler seldom reveals himself over the water. Some perfectionists even disguise themselves with netting and tufts of vegetation. They may look strange, but any precaution that enables the angler to catch more fish is worth considering. Far better to go to this extreme than to risk going fishless through neglecting to take reasonable precautions.

METHODS OF STREAM FISHING

The Way of the Hunter

Basically, there are two methods which can be used to catch fish from small streams. One is the familiar method of ground-baiting a swim, and then fishing it with a bait presented on either float or leger tackle. The other method is not so well-known and is certainly not used by the majority of anglers, but it is perhaps one of the most effective methods of catching fish from small waters. Instead of sitting over one swim, the angler takes his rod and baits and goes in search of the fish. He does not use groundbait habitually, or burden himself with a lot of equipment. His weapons are stealth, a sound knowledge of the water and its fish, a keenly observant eye, and the ability to cast accurately.

In this sense he becomes a hunter, rather than a passive spectator. The old idea of waiting patiently over a swim for the fish to 'come on', has little relevance to this style of fishing. The angler does not remain long in any one place, but is constantly on the move. Most of the fish he catches fall to his first cast, so that his aim must always be to take them by surprise. It is an intensely absorbing kind of fishing and especially deadly when the water is low and clear.

Extreme stealth is essential when using this method. Fish in streams are easily alarmed, and as alarm spreads rapidly throughout a swim, the noisy angler will seldom catch many fish. But the angler who has learned to move quietly, and avoids even letting his shadow fall across the water, will rarely be disappointed.

There are few species of fish which cannot be caught by using this hunting style of angling, though certain species, such as trout, chub, perch, and pike, are caught more often than others. It is significant that all these species are predatory: that is, they feed mainly on other, smaller fish. For predators all respond more readily to a moving bait, or to a bait that is *alive*, whereas such fish as roach, rudd, dace, and bream are seldom caught with

live-baits, and usually need more time than predators to pick up
the bait.

With Float or Leger

There are, of course, some swims unsuited to the hunting
style of angling and where it is possible, or even preferable, for
the angler to remain static and to float-fish, or leger, his bait
downstream. If this style is adopted the angler should still try
to remain concealed, and *downstream* of the fish wherever possible.
Many anglers ruin their immediate chances by walking upstream,
close to the edge of the stream, when it would be wiser to arrive
at their chosen position by making a detour. It is often the first
cast, or the first swim down, that catches the biggest fish, and it
is foolish to ruin this opportunity by standing directly over the
swim. A good practice is to fish upstream first, casting the bait
into every accessible spot, and only when all possibilities of
catching a fish quickly have been exhausted to turn to the waiting
game.

Even then, fishing should never be allowed to become a dull
routine, and the successful stream angler should always be ready
to improvise, and to adapt his methods and baits to the needs
of the moment. Fish—and especially specimen fish—are not always
willing to feed at once; and when they are not the angler must be
prepared to wait, and perhaps to encourage them to start feeding
by careful and selective groundbaiting. This kind of fishing
demands qualities of patience and endurance which all anglers do
not possess, but there can be no doubt that it can be rewarding,
provided the angler persists in his chosen swim.

In the course of time he will gradually learn which swims are
most likely to produce fish by the waiting method, and which
species of fish are most likely to respond to it. Generally speaking,
the larger and deeper the swim the more likely it is that it will
contain a lot of fish, and such a swim is often best fished with a
float or leger. Most of the fish caught in this way will be shoal
fish, such as roach, rudd, and bream; but chub, perch, and pike
are often caught with float or leger, too. The angler must decide
which method is best suited to the particular character of each

swim, bearing in mind always the *kind* of fish he is hoping to catch.

Being of a somewhat restless nature, my own preference, on most occasions is for the hunting style of angling which I find more interesting and more rewarding. It also permits the methods of angling—upstream worming, spinning, and fly-fishing—that I most enjoy, and gives one the feeling of *participating*, angling in the full sense of the word.

SELECTIVE ANGLING

The true angler, as distinct from the novice who merely baits a hook and casts it hopefully into the water, is the man who knows what he wants to catch, who understands fish, and angles for each species exclusively. One day he might angle for roach; the next for perch. On other occasions he will prefer to go for chub, pike, or rudd. But always he fishes selectively rather than indiscriminately.

Naturally, it is much easier to angle indiscriminately, and to catch any fish that might happen to take the bait. Selective angling is more difficult. The angler must first learn about the fish, their habits, the swims where they are most likely to be found, and the baits they are most likely to take. Only then can he begin to fish for each species with any confidence. Later it will be explained, in more detail, how this selectivity can be applied to the different species of fish, but the basic principles of selective fishing should perhaps be stated now, for they form the basis of what constitutes real angling, as distinct from mere fishing.

The first essential is to locate the fish. Nothing else the angler does is as important; nothing else he does will influence the end result so strongly. If his knowledge of the stream is full and complete, this will be the easiest part of the operation and will enormously increase his chances of catching the fish he has selected. If that knowledge is lacking, he will be handicapped right from the start.

The next step is to choose a selective bait—one which the chosen species is most likely to take at any given time. If, for instance, a shoal of dace can be seen rising, an artificial fly, or a chrysalid, would be the most obvious choice of bait. If, on the other hand, pike were the quarry, a live fish would be preferable. These may seem obvious choices, but it is surprising how many anglers fail to give sufficient thought to this matter.

Choosing the most favourable time to seek each species is also important. Some are caught more readily when the water is coloured. For others, when the water is low, dawn and dusk are often the best times to seek them. Certain swims produce more fish when the water is high; others fish better when the water is running at normal, or low level. The angler who has acquired this knowledge, and puts it to use, will catch the species of fish he is after far more often than the angler who relies upon luck and chance to carry him through.

3

Tackle

CHOOSING THE RODS

EVERY angler fishes best with tackle which he feels is right for him. There is a 'feel' about a rod that is difficult to explain, but which any experienced angler can recognise instinctively. Therefore, one can only give general guidance as to the *type* of rod most likely to be suitable for different styles of fishing. Theoretically, it should be possible to manage with just one all-purpose rod but, in practice, the differing requirements imposed by the nature of the water and the style of fishing to be used, have also to be taken into consideration. Bearing in mind that many streams are narrow and overgrown, a powerful rod, capable of handling a big fish in difficult conditions, is obviously essential. Such a rod can be used for upstream worming, and for legering, but is not suitable for float-fishing with fine lines. The keen all-rounder will also find use for a spinning rod, a fly-rod, and a pike rod.

The most important of these rods is undoubtedly the one which can be used for legering, and for handling large fish in difficult swims. Since it can also be used for light spinning, it is the most versatile of all the rods, and the one which I use more than any other. Ideally, such a rod should not be too long; it should be capable of handling a large fish, and casting a large bait on a strong line. It should also be light, as the angler will be holding it continually. A long, heavy rod would impose too much strain on his casting arm.

Many years ago such a rod would have been difficult to obtain. Now many excellent rods are obtainable in either built-cane or fibreglass. My own choice is for the Mark IV Carp rod, which is 10ft long, has a test-curve of 1lb, and can be used in conjunction with lines of between 6 and 12lb breaking-strain. The Mark IV Avon, though not as powerful, is also an excellent rod for fishing with lines of between 3 and 7lb breaking-strain.

The lower figure indicates the minimum line strength that should be used with each rod, but rather than run the risk of a breakage, I prefer to play safe and have found a line of between 5–6lb breaking-strain ideal for the Mark IV Avon rod, and a line between 7–8lb breaking-strain best for the Mark IV Carp.

A larger rod is sometimes useful for reaching out over reed-beds, and for this reason some anglers prefer to use a traditional 11ft Avon rod, or one of the longer, stepped-up carp rods that are now obtainable; but I would not recommend any angler to use a rod over 12ft long for legering, or for hunting big fish. A rod of this length is too cumbersome for upstream fishing, and often too floppy for legering, or for stopping the supercharged rush of a big fish in time to prevent it from gaining the shelter of a reed-bed or snag.

Rods of between 12 and 14ft, which can be used with lines of a lower breaking-strain, are useful for float-fishing in the more open swims, especially when fishing for roach, dace, bream, and rudd. My own favourite rod for this type of fishing is 12ft long, and can be used with lines as low as 1½lb breaking-strain. It is much softer in action than the Mark IV rods, and allows one to fish quite delicately under conditions which would prohibit the use of strong lines and heavy tackle.

The other rods are not essential, but do enable the angler to widen his range and to fish with the most suitable tackle for each different style of fishing. They include a light spinning rod, for spinning with small spinners and spoons; a fly-rod for both dry-fly and wet-fly fishing; and a pike rod which can be used for live-baiting and dead-baiting, or for spinning with large spinners and spoons. I use an 8½ft built-cane rod for light spinning; an 8ft fly-rod for fly-fishing and upstreaming in overgrown places; and a 10ft pike rod. It is not necessary, or desirable, of course, to carry all these rods, and one should decide beforehand what style of fishing one intends to use, and then carry one rod, at the most two, to the waterside. Fishing overgrown streams can be a tiring business, and the less unnecessary equipment one carries the better.

CHOOSING THE REEL

There is no doubt in my mind that the fixed-spool reel is far superior to any other type of reel for fishing in overgrown streams. It has the great advantage that the line can be cast directly from the reel, whereas on the centre-pin reel—admittedly useful for long-trotting work—the line has to be pulled from the reel with the left hand before the bait can be cast.

There are many excellent fixed-spool reels on the market now, and one which has a high gear ratio, so that it will recover line quickly, is obviously useful for upstream worming, and for spinning. Whatever the reel, it is always essential to fill the spool with line to within $\frac{1}{8}$in of its lip—but not more. If the spool is *too* full 'bird's nests' of line are likely to result when the cast is made. If it is not filled to the recommended mark it will not be possible to cast smoothly, or accurately. Prior attention to this small but important point, will prevent much unnecessary trouble and wasted time on the bank. A fly-reel capable of holding about 50yd of line is also useful if the angler intends to fish with a fly. Certain kinds of fly-fishing are possible with ordinary rods and lines, but the proper equipment is essential for fishing the fly in the traditional manner.

MATCHING THE LINE TO THE ROD

The fine lines suitable for use in canals and still-waters will not be strong enough for fishing overgrown streams, and for these I seldom use a line of less than 3lb breaking-strain, except for surface fishing for dace, or when fishing for roach in a snag-free swim. For these I use a line of around 2lb breaking-strain; but most of my fishing is done with lines of between 3 and 8lb breaking-strain.

It is all-important that the line should be matched to the rod;

and also that the line should be strong enough to make landing a fish more of a certainty than a mere possibility. It is futile to use a strong line on a rod that is not suited to that line strength. Each must complement the other and work in unison, just as does any other properly adjusted piece of equipment. If, for instance, I intend to fish for chub in a snaggy swim I would use a 7–8lb breaking-strain line and my Mark IV Carp rod, knowing that with this equipment I could handle any chub I might hook without fear of the line breaking—unless it had developed an undetected weakness. In this type of swim a 3–4lb line would be inadequate, and I would use it only in a snag-free swim, and with the Mark IV Avon rod. This tackle could also be used for roach or perch fishing in difficult swims; but if the swim were free of snags I would use my roach rod and a line of 2–3lb breaking-strain.

The strength of the tackle lies in the correct matching of rod and line, and if this has not been achieved it is liable to be found wanting when the 'moment of truth' arrives, resulting in a broken line and a lost fish. So, make a point of always using the strongest tackle you think is necessary, taking into account the prevailing conditions and the probable size of the fish. One does not need a lot of imagination to appreciate the strain placed on the tackle by a large chub or pike, hooked in a difficult, overgrown swim. In stream fishing, unlike still-water or canal fishing, conditions often favour the fish, so the wise angler makes sure that his tackle will be strong enough to hold the largest fish he is likely to catch. It does, of course, sometimes happen that large fish are hooked when one is fishing for roach or dace with a line of low breaking-strain, but such incidents must be accepted as occupational hazards and will serve to emphasise the importance of always seeking large fish with strong tackle.

If a very fine line is used, it should only be when the angler knows that he has a reasonable chance of landing any fish he hooks. If, for example, one was fishing for roach or dace in exceptionally clear water with a line of only 1lb breaking-strain, the weakness of the line should be offset by a rod capable of absorbing most of the strain put upon the line. A fly-rod is ideal for this type of fishing as it is so pliable that the line is seldom tested to the limit of its strength. This kind of tackle should, however, be used only in exceptional circumstances, and never when fishing for big fish.

Many anglers avoid using strong lines because they think that the thickness of the line will scare the fish and prevent them from taking the bait; but this is rarely true. Only when the water is very clear and low, or when a slow-sinking style is used, does it become advisable to use the finer line. When the water is coloured, it is seldom necessary to use a line of low breaking-strain. Indeed, taking into account the increased force of the current and the probable size of the fish, it would be foolhardy to do so.

HOOKS

The main requirement of a hook is that it should be sharp and strong. The hooks I prefer are straight-eyed hooks, in sizes 14 to 1, and most of my stream fishing is done with the larger hooks, fished on a strong line. A large hook should never be used on a line of low breaking-strain, and the larger the bait is, the larger the hook should be. Large hooks give a firmer hold and are easier to extract than smaller ones. Gilt, spade-end hooks should never be used on a strong line as they are likely to straighten out when a big fish is hooked and exerts a strong pull on the tackle. Such hooks should only be used with fine lines and a supple rod, and for fishing for the smaller fish, such as roach, rudd, bream and dace.

FLOATS

A small selection of floats should be carried when stream fishing as there are times when they are useful. Specialised floats are not required; the needs of the stream angler can be met with a few large floats for heavy water fishing, and a range of smaller floats for fishing when the water is at or below normal level. A few swan, goose, or large porcupine quills will suffice for spate fishing, and a few small porcupine or fowl quills for low-water fishing. The very small floats will only be used for roach, or dace. A float capable of supporting a large live-bait could also be included for pike fishing.

Usually, however, it is best to fish without a float—especially in those small, clear streams where the appearance of a float on the water might scare the fish. If, on occasion, a float is deemed necessary, a small twig can be used to carry the bait downstream. A 'float' of this type looks more natural, and is less likely to scare the fish.

Floats, in general, should be dull in colour—preferably brown or green—and the tip should be yellow or orange, as these two colours are most easily seen against the dark background that is normal in most stream fishing.

WEIGHTS

A selection of split-shot, ranging in size from tiny dust-shot to swan-shot, should always be carried. These weights will be used mainly for float-fishing methods, and for light legering. Leger-weights are essential to the small stream and a selection of these, up to $\frac{1}{2}$oz, should always be carried. The larger weights will be useful for legering in heavy, or fast-flowing water, and the smaller ones for legering in normal, or low-water conditions.

OTHER TACKLE NEEDS

Anglers often tend to overburden themselves with tackle; and particularly when fishing streams, where the accent is usually on mobility, it is best to travel as lightly as possible and to carry only essential equipment. Other useful items of equipment are a landing-net, a keep-net, a gaff for pike, a selection of wire traces for spinning and live-baiting, a selection of swivels, a pair of artery forceps for extracting hooks, a bait-can for retaining small live-baits, and, if desired, a basket, stool or plastic sheet to sit on. Leave all unessential equipment in a safe place on the bank if you are adopting the 'hunting' method of angling and always remember to try and stay concealed, or at least to keep as low to the ground as possible.

4

Baits

UNDOUBTEDLY, the best all-round bait for stream fishing is the worm. It is one of the deadliest baits for chub, perch, and trout; most other species will also take it, and even pike are sometimes tempted by a large worm.

The big lobworm can be found in most gardens, as long as the soil is damp; but the best places to find it are on bowling-greens, tennis-courts, cricket-pitches—or anywhere where the grass is short enough to permit the worm to be seen. During the day it is rarely seen on the surface, but at night large quantities can often be picked up with the aid of a torch. The light should never be shone directly on to the worm though, or it will quickly retreat into its hole. The best time to seek lobworms is after a long period of heavy rain, when the ground has been thoroughly soaked. They can also be bought from suppliers.

Once obtained, they should be placed in a large receptacle, such as a discarded bath, or a large bowl, half-filled with a mixture of damp soil and vegetation. Leaf mould, or grass tussocks are ideal. Never fill the receptacle to the brim, or the worms will escape. If the soil in the container is dampened by periodic sprinkling with water, the worms can be kept indefinitely.

Some anglers use only the tail of the lobworm, others, like myself, prefer to use the whole worm. Because of its size, this type of worm should always be fished on a large hook, preferably a size 4, or 6, and certainly no smaller than a size 10. The hook should be inserted once only, and closer to the head than the tail.

It is a mistake to thread the worm on the hook as this reduces its liveliness and makes it less attractive to the fish.

The smaller red-worms, or brandlings, which can be found abundantly in rotted-down manure heaps, are also useful. Although they lack the size and weight of the lobworm, they are an excellent bait for most species of fish—especially for perch. Unfortunately, they are also very attractive to minnows, and when these nuisance fish are troublesome the bigger lobworm should be used. Brandlings should be fished on a smaller hook than the lobworm—a size 10 or 12 is about right—or a bunch of them can be fished on a larger hook, when required.

Two other types of worm are also worth mentioning. One is a tough, pinkish-coloured worm that can often be found in gardens, but is more plentiful in chicken-runs, or anywhere where poultry are allowed to run free. This worm is smaller than the lobworm, but larger than the brandling, and can be a deadly bait when upstreaming for trout.

The other is a big worm with a characteristic bluish-red sheen on its body, which can be found along the banks of some rivers after a flood. It lies beneath tussocks of grass and debris and, if used in the river beside which it is found, is often irresistible to all fish—probably because they have become accustomed to eating it after the floods have washed it into the river.

Worms of all types can be used in most water conditions, but are most effective during and after a spate, when the water is high and coloured.

BREAD-BAITS

Bread-baits come next in order of importance to the stream angler, and have the advantage of being easily obtainable, clean to handle, and capable of preparation in several different ways. The only species of fish that seldom takes them are pike and perch. All others will take bread-baits, and they are exceptionally good for roach and rudd.

The three forms of bread most commonly used are flake, crust, and paste. It would be difficult to separate them into any order of effectiveness as each is an excellent bait and the angler should be prepared to use them all as conditions dictate.

Flake

Flake, which is the inside of a new loaf, is simply torn from the loaf and squeezed gently around the shank of the hook. Stale loaves should be avoided as the inside is too dry and crumbly, and a freshly-baked loaf of the kind known as a tin-loaf is best. The size of the flake used varies, according to the water conditions and to the species of fish being sought. In general, small pieces, mounted on a size 10 or 12 hook, should be used for roach, rudd, and dace; but it is not possible to lay down any precise rules. There are occasions when all fish will accept the larger pieces of flake, fished on a size 6, or even a size 4 hook. For chub, there can be little doubt that, on most occasions, a large piece of flake is more effective than a small piece. I seldom use pieces of less than thumb-nail size, and have caught chub with pieces the size of a small orange, fished on a size 1 hook. Flake is seldom of much use in spate conditions, but is most effective when the water is clear and slow-moving—possibly because it covers the hook entirely and sinks very slowly.

Crust

Crust is one of the finest baits for chub, large roach, and large dace. The best kind of crust is the golden-coloured part taken from the sides and bottom of the loaf. Some anglers prepare it by keeping it in a damp cloth and cutting it into cubes, but I prefer simply to tear off a rough fragment from the loaf. Unlike flake, crust cannot be squeezed around the hook, and must be mounted by passing the point of the hook through the bait. I do not think it matters if the point is left revealed.

The actual size of the crust used depends mainly upon the species of fish being sought. For roach and dace a piece about the size of a finger-nail, mounted on a size 8 hook, is about right. For chub, a piece at least as big as a 10p-piece should be used. There may be occasions when a smaller piece is to be preferred but, in general, the larger the crust the more likely it is that a chub will take it. This fact should be kept in mind, because the size of the bait often plays an important part in determining which species of fish will be caught.

Like flake, crust is an effective bait for low-water fishing, but is most deadly during the after-spate period when the water is fining down and clearing. As it is a more buoyant bait than either flake or paste, more weight is needed to sink it.

Paste

This bait is heavier than the other two, but is no less effective as a bait for chub, roach, rudd, and dace; and has the added advantage of being more durable, and therefore less likely to disintegrate on the hook through the action of the current. It can be fished in a slow-sinking style, but is more suited to bottom fishing—provided that the bottom is free of weeds or other debris. In swims complicated by weeds it is better to use the more buoyant flake, or crust, both of which will remain visible above the weeds. Paste is especially useful in the fast-flowing swims where, because of its greater weight, it will sink more quickly.

Unlike the other two bread-baits, paste must be prepared, and care in its preparation is all-important. If the paste is too hard the fish will find it unpalatable and reject it. If it is too soft it will either fly off the hook when the cast is made, or rapidly disintegrate on impact with the water. The best paste is made from the inside of a *stale* loaf, which should be soaked and then pressed in a cloth until it becomes soft but firm. It should not be sloppy, or crumbly. A perfect paste can be easily moulded around a hook, and will not fly off during casting. If anything, it is better to err slightly on the side of having the paste too soft, rather than too hard. Like the other bread-baits, it can be fished in a variety of sizes. I generally fish it on a size 8 or 10 hook for roach, but at least a size 4 when seeking chub.

Some anglers add flavouring to the paste to make it more attractive to the fish, but whether it really does so is a debatable point. It is, however, true that fish are able to detect food by smell, so it is possible that a flavouring of aniseed, hempseed, or some other atttractive scent, could make a bait more palatable.

It can certainly do no harm, and could serve to mask other less attractive human odours which might deter the fish from taking the paste.

CHEESE

During the summer, when the hordes of minnows are most active, it is often better to use cheese instead of bread-baits, as it withstands the attacks of these voracious little fish much longer. As a bait it is most effective for chub, and sometimes for roach, too. Other species are not often caught with this bait, so that I tend to use it almost exclusively for chub.

The consistency and flavour of the cheese are more important than its colour. Any highly-flavoured cheese, such as Cheddar, Lancashire, or Danish Blue, can be used. Some cheeses are soft enough to permit them to be moulded around the hook. Others are too hard, or too crumbly, and must be broken up and blended with water to form a soft paste. A mixture of stale bread and cheese: or even better, bread-dough and cheese, is equally effective. The latter mixture has the advantage of being soft, but is of such elastic consistency that it stays on the hook much better than cheese alone does. Processed cheese can also be used, but tends to harden in the water.

There seems little point in fishing this bait on a small hook, and I rarely use a hook of smaller than size 10 for roach fishing, and a size 4 when seeking chub. Chub can gulp in a bait as big as a bantam's egg quite easily, and even one this size does not always deter other, smaller fish from taking it.

MAGGOTS

Maggots are much too attractive to small fish such as minnows, sticklebacks, bullheads and gudgeon to make an ideal bait, and only during the winter, when interference from minnows is negligible, do they become really useful and can be used to catch roach, dace, rudd, bream, perch, and even chub. In streams where minnows are not numerous the maggot will naturally be much

31

more effective, but it is by no means as selective as the other baits previously mentioned.

Since a large, lively maggot is more attractive to fish than a small, half-dead one, it is advisable to use small, sharp hooks and to hook the maggot lightly through the skin, close to its rear end. It will then stay lively for a reasonable length of time. As soon as it begins to look lifeless, or when it has been sampled and rejected by a fish, it should be removed from the hook and a fresh one attached.

Fresh maggots are greasy, and often have an unpleasant odour, so that it is advisable to clean them before use by allowing them to work through bran or sawdust. They should always be given plenty of room, and kept in a large tin which has a lid perforated by numerous small holes. Be careful not to make the holes too large or the maggots will escape. All maggots can be coloured by using special dyes, but there is little evidence to suggest that coloured maggots are any more attractive than the normal white, or yellow ones.

The smallness of this bait means that it cannot normally be fished on a large hook. Most anglers use a size 14, or 16; but a larger hook can be used to fish a bunch of maggots on the bottom —in which case a size 10, or 12, is preferable.

CHRYSALIDS

Chrysalids, which are the pupae of maggots, are often a more effective bait than the maggots themselves. Chub, roach and rudd, will take them and, as a surface-fished bait to catch dace, a chrysalid cannot be bettered.

This bait has been used by discerning anglers for a long time, but only in recent years has it become well-known—mainly through the publicity given to it by match anglers. In the process, the chrysalid has acquired a new name, and is now often known as a caster. In their early stages of development chrysalids are a pale yellow colour. Later, they darken to redbrown; and finally, to black. In their early stages casters will sink under their own weight and the angler who wishes to acquire a quantity of them should first buy a supply of maggots and allow them to 'turn', a process which can be hastened by keeping them in a warm place. The chrysalids should then be placed in a bucket of water, and those that float skimmed off. Those that sink are the casters and should be used immediately. If it is wished to retain them for a day or so, they must be kept in a cold place— a refrigerator would be ideal if the angler's wife will allow him to use it. The chrysalids that float are usually in a more advanced stage of growth than the casters, and are often thrown away. This is a mistake, because floaters are one of the most deadly baits for dace that can be obtained.

Casters can be fished in a slow-sinking style without using any additional weight, and are generally fished on a small, fine-wire hook, size 16, or 18. Floaters must also be mounted on a small hook. Two methods of attaching the bait are generally used. One is to attach the chrysalid as one attaches a maggot—with the hook lightly piercing the blunt end. The other is to conceal the hook completely inside the chrysalid, and this method is preferable when the fish are biting shyly.

Both forms of chrysalids can be used right through the season, but floaters are more effective during the summer and autumn when fish are more likely to be feeding at surface level. Casters, fished hard on the bottom, or in a slow-sinking style, are most effective when there are no signs of surface activity.

SEED-BAITS

These baits, which include wheat, malt, hempseed, maize, and pearl-barley, can all be used to catch most species of fish, the only exceptions being perch and pike. They are especially deadly for roach, and to a lesser degree for chub. I use them extensively during the summer and autumn months.

Wheat

Wheat is probably the best known of these baits, is quite cheap, and can be obtained from any corn merchant. Preparation is important if the best results are to be obtained, and my own method is to soak the wheat for at least twenty-four hours, then to transfer it to a large saucepan, cover it with water, and simmer it very slowly for several hours. The wheat is ready for use when the grains are swollen to approximately twice their original size, and have split open to reveal a firm, white centre.

Traditionally, wheat is supposed to be most effective around harvest time, but can be used equally well throughout the summer and autumn. A size 12 hook is about right for wheat, with a larger hook if several grains are being used at the same time.

Malt

Malt was used as a bait at least as far back as the seventeenth century, but is not widely known to present-day anglers—possibly because it is not as easy to obtain as some other baits. Malt is roasted barley, and is used in the making of beer. Like wheat, it should be soaked before cooking, and then simmered slowly for several hours in a saucepan until the grains become well-swollen and reveal a firm, white centre. An alternative method, for a smaller quantity, is to cook it in a vacuum flask.

Malt is an excellent bait for roach, but will also lure chub, dace, and bream. During the summer, it can often be used to single out roach, which respond to it more readily than any other stream fish. It can be fished in a slow-sinking style, or on the bottom. A size 16 hook should be used to fish one grain: size 10, or 12, for two or more grains.

An important point to remember about all seed-baits is that they sink quickly and do not disintegrate. Large quantities should not, therefore, be thrown into the swim, or the fish will rapidly become satiated with the seeds and more difficult to catch. Try throwing a handful or two into the swim to attract the fish and encourage them to start feeding; after which a few grains, tossed in at intervals, should be sufficient.

NATURAL BAITS

From the Land

In their search for a killing bait anglers are apt to overlook the most obvious ones—the baits that can be found in and around the water, and which form a large part of the natural diet of fish. These baits are deadly in small rivers and streams, where the confined nature of the water permits the angler to make a much closer approach to the fish, and to present his bait to it.

One of the most useful of natural baits is the small black beetle that can be found under stones, fallen branches, and other debris. On a hot summer day this insect will often lure a chub or trout if it is dangled carefully on the surface. Grasshoppers are another excellent bait, although they are not as common as they once were, and not easy to catch. A child's fishing-net or a butterfly-net is a useful weapon for catching these insects. Either should be mounted on a size 8, or size 10 hook, and fished on the surface. The hook should never be thrust through the body of the insect, but through its wing-case. It will then stay lively for a long time.

In the mornings, when there is a heavy dew on the grass, the black slug can often be found, and there are few better baits than this one for chub. It is, in fact, one of the most selective baits one can use, since few other species will accept it. The smaller slugs are also useful baits, but the big black ones are easily the best and should be fished on a big hook. A size 4, or size 2, is none too large.

The various kinds of caterpillars which can be found along the banks of most streams are also acceptable baits for most species of fish. A sharp, size 12 hook should be used and I have caught roach, chub, dace, perch, and even gudgeon with caterpillars.

From Beneath the Water
Beneath the water lies perhaps the richest supply of natural baits. The largest of these is the crayfish—although it is not found in all waters. Like the slug, it is a very selective bait inasmuch as it is mainly used to catch chub. Large perch and pike will occasionally take a crayfish, but very rarely are any other fish caught with it. It is quite possible, however, that baby crayfish would be a useful bait for roach, perch, and dace. Adult crayfish are quite large, and should be fished on a size 2 hook,

or even a size 1. The crayfish should be killed with a sharp blow before use, otherwise, once it has landed in the water, it will scuttle away into hiding.

Caddis-grubs are another bait which will catch many different species of fish, and are quite easy to obtain. In appearance, they resemble small pieces of stick, and can often be seen crawling slowly along the bottom in shallow parts of a stream. It is not necessary to remove the outer cases in order to use them. As with most natural baits, the best results are obtained when the grub is presented to a visible fish, but they can be fished on float tackle which is set to allow the grub to trip slowly across the bottom.

The tiny freshwater shrimp exists in vast quantities in most streams, and can easily be caught with a child's fishing-net. Like most natural baits, they will not always tempt fish; but when roach can be seen feeding on them the opportunity should not be missed, as specimen fish have been caught with this bait. The shrimp is equally effective for dace, trout and rudd and should be fished on a very small, sharp hook, size 16 or 18.

FLIES

Many kinds of flies can be seen along the banks of streams during the summer; but most of them are too difficult to catch whereas bluebottles and house-flies—both most attractive baits to chub and dace—are easily obtained by allowing a quantity of maggots to hatch out into flies. Fish them on the surface on a floating line and a small, sharp hook, size 12; though there are occasions when they are even more effective if fished beneath the surface.

Other flies, such as dragon-flies, damsel-flies, and crane-flies (daddy-long-legs), are all excellent baits for trout, chub, and dace; but they are now rather scarce and difficult to obtain.

OTHER FISH

In the world of fish there is a constant struggle for survival, and fierce competition for food. Small fish, such as minnows, gudgeon, bleak, loach, bullheads, and dace, together with the fry of all other species, are all consumed by the larger fish. These, in turn, are consumed by the true predators: pike, chub, perch, and trout.

Small bait fish should not, therefore, be overlooked by any angler and the most important of these and the one most frequently to be found is the minnow. It is prolific in most rivers and streams, and is an ideal bait for chub, perch, trout, and to a lesser degree, for pike. The larger fish, such as gudgeon, loach, dace, and roach, are also eaten by chub and perch, but are more commonly used as a bait for pike.

Obviously, then, no angler ever needs to restrict himself to a single bait, though it would be foolish indeed to try all baits in the hope that an infallible one would eventually be found. Each bait is most effective when it is chosen specifically to catch a certain species of fish, and used at the time and place most suited to that purpose.

5

Groundbaiting

ITS USES AND MIS-USES

GROUNDBAIT has several functions: to attract fish into a swim, to start them feeding, and as a means of introducing them to a different bait. Depending upon the type of groundbait used, it can also have an influence on the species of fish caught, and upon their size. The angler who has fished observantly, and knows where to find each species, will seldom need to use groundbait to attract fish. Instead, his knowledge of the water will enable him to take his bait to the fish. For this reason, and because of the smallness of the majority of the swims, I believe that groundbait is of limited value in small rivers and streams.

So strong, though, is the influence of tradition and habit, that many anglers would not think of going fishing without groundbait. True, there are times, and occasions, when groundbait can increase one's chances of catching fish, as will later be explained; but it is a mistake to assume that it is *always* necessary to use it. In fact, it could be said that the angler who always uses groundbait not only often ruins his immediate chances, but also demonstrates that he has not really studied the art of stream fishing. He cloaks his lack of knowledge of the water by using groundbait to lure the fish to him. Sometimes he succeeds: more often he does not. Better, then, to decide first when and under what circumstances groundbait should be used, and then, if possible, to use it in such a way as to increase one's chances of catching a particular species of fish. It is neither wise nor good angling to use groundbait indiscriminately, or merely from force of habit.

The style of fishing I usually adopt—moving gradually up-stream and casting my bait into every likely swim—is not usually associated with groundbaiting, because it depends almost entirely for its success on the element of surprise. To stand over the swim and throw groundbait in would almost certainly ruin any immediate chance of success, even though any fish thus disturbed might later return to that swim. Instead, by fishing up the stream, always moving stealthily along the bank, I am often able to take fish without using a scrap of groundbait; and it is no accident that a large percentage of these fish are often good big ones.

As these tactics have shown that they will catch fish more often than not I now groundbait only when it is really necessary, usually when I have decided to concentrate on one swim. Even then, I always cast my bait up into the swim first, on the assumption that a good fish might be lying there awaiting any scrap of food that may come down to it on the current.

Another factor which often makes groundbait superfluous is that the fish might already be in a feeding mood, and do not need any further encouragement to feed. Whether this is so or not can quickly be ascertained by trying the swim with the bait. If bites develop quickly and regularly—as they sometimes do—there is no need to use groundbait. Fish do not feed all the time, but in cycles dictated by their need for food. When this need becomes imperative they begin to search for food, and can sometimes be observed doing so. Watching shoals of roach in clear and shallow swims, it is often possible to determine whether they are feeding or merely drifting idly to and fro.

If they are feeding, groundbaiting is usually unnecessary; but if they show little interest in a proffered bait, groundbaiting—of the right kind—may encourage them to start. Fish are ruled by instinct, and once one begins to feed the other members of the shoal will often follow suit.

If fish are not already feeding groundbaiting is unlikely to bring about a quick change as they will usually need time to sample the groundbait before starting to feed on it. Knowing this, I usually bait up a chosen swim on my way upstream and then return to it later. Sometimes I bait up several swims and fish each in turn as I come back downstream. Sometimes only one swim yields fish. At other times perhaps two or more will. More rarely, the groundbait has no effect, and no fish are caught. When that happens, one must accept that the fish are not going to start feeding, and turn to other swims, or perhaps to a different style of fishing altogether.

TYPES OF GROUNDBAIT

Most groundbaits are composed of fine particles of crushed bread and meal, and disintegrate rapidly when thrown into the swim. The idea is that the groundbait will attract, but not feed. In slow-moving water the cloud effect caused by the slow disintegration of the groundbait will linger for quite a long time, and can be enhanced by adding powdered milk, or by soaking the groundbait in milk. This type of groundbait is most attractive to the smaller fish, such as dace, roach, rudd, and the smaller fry of the larger fish, such as chub and bream. It is of limited value as a means of attracting fish in fast water because it disintegrates too quickly. A heavier, more durable form of groundbait must be used in this type of swim; so it is made heavier by increasing the amount of solid matter in the mixture, or by using a higher proportion of heavy meal. It can be made to sink even more quickly by compressing it into compact balls which sink rapidly before breaking up.

Groundbaits which disintegrate quickly are apt to be too attractive to small fish to be of much value to the stream angler who wishes to catch the larger fish. If that is his aim, he should refrain from using groundbait altogether, or use a groundbait composed of more substantial particles of the hook-bait, which are more likely to interest the larger fish. Small fish feed mainly upon tiny organisms. The larger fish, having passed through this stage, often seek bigger items of food, which they find mainly on the bottom, or in the weeds.

These bigger fish are sometimes attracted by fine groundbait, but the competition from smaller fish, especially minnows, is often so intense that they are prevented from taking their share.

If, on the other hand, a groundbait composed of larger, more solid particles is used, smaller fish are not able to swallow it easily, and the larger fish are then more likely to command their share. Thus, by using a different, heavier type of groundbait, it is possible to catch a greater proportion of bigger fish, and even to catch more of one species of fish than any other—provided the angler uses his knowledge of the water to ensure that he is fishing where he has the best chance of catching the species he has in view.

SELECTIVE GROUNDBAITING

The first essential of all successful angling is accurate location. The groundbait, angling method, and bait are then selected so that the angler is always fishing in the manner most likely to lure the species of fish he is seeking. If, for instance, chub are the quarry, the groundbait should contain a large proportion of solid matter. Chub are large fish with capacious mouths, and when they are feeding well they have ravenous appetites. Small particles of food do not usually interest them. If a bread-based groundbait is used, it should contain large pieces of soaked flake or crust. If cheese or paste is the hook bait, then the groundbait should consist mainly of pieces of these baits. Worms should be thrown in whole. This type of groundbait is far more likely to bring chub on the feed than the fine cloud variety of groundbait.

No matter what type of groundbait is used, it should never be thrown into that part of a swim where chub have been located. Instead, the angler should conceal himself as best he can at the head of the swim, and make use of the current to carry the groundbait naturally downstream to the chub. By doing this he will avoid scaring them, and at the same time encourage them to accept the bait he intends to catch them with.

The effect this kind of groundbaiting can have on chub is sometimes startling. Swims which once seemed empty may suddenly become alive with activity as the chub begin feeding, and fish after fish may be caught during such a period. Much, of course, depends on the size of the swim, and the care which the angler takes to avoid frightening the shoal when he extracts his fish.

Roach and rudd, which usually move about in much larger shoals than chub, often need encouraging to feed, and the most effective groundbait for both species is one composed of soaked flake or crust. This should be introduced into the swim in the same careful manner as when groundbaiting for chub. Bread is possibly the most selective form of groundbait for roach and rudd, but a groundbait composed of either malt, wheat, or hempseed, is also very effective for bringing roach on the feed.

Perch do not respond to a bread-based groundbait at all, and are best attracted by one consisting of broken worms. If these are dropped carefully into the swim, or—where the water is fast-moving—encased in a ball of clay, it is often possible to encourage perch to start feeding. This may take some time, and the angler should not leave the swim if the perch do not begin feeding at once. On many occasions I have had to wait several hours for perch to begin feeding; but once they do start it is often possible to catch a lot within a comparatively short time. Much seems to depend on the height and colour of the water, and the lower and clearer it is, the more difficult it is to coax the perch to feed. The best time is just after a spate, when the perch are hungry and actively seeking food.

Bream are a bottom-loving fish, and this should be kept in mind when making up a groundbait for them. It should generally be heavy, so that it will sink quickly and not break up until it reaches the bottom. A mixture of equal parts of bread-crumbs and wheatmeal, into which has been blended a liberal supply of brandlings or maggots, is one of the best groundbaits for bream. Of all stream fish, bream respond best to groundbaiting, and it is rare to catch any quantity of them without using some form of groundbait to start them feeding.

Dace respond to almost any of the fine groundbaits mentioned, and it is not at all unusual to catch them when fishing for roach or rudd. But the most effective groundbait for dace, and certainly the most selective, is one consisting almost entirely of chrysalids. If these are fed steadily into a swim which is known to hold dace the majority of the fish caught will be dace. Groundbait is not often used for other species, such as pike, trout and, where present, sea-trout or salmon. Pike are often lured by other fish which have been attracted by the angler's groundbait, but all these species are generally sought by methods which do not involve groundbaiting techniques.

6

Angling for Trout

THE NATURE OF THE FISH

MARCH, a month of steely grey skies, sweeping rain, and freshly budding trees, ushers in the trout season; and by the time the hawthorns are in full bloom trout can often be seen rising to sip in flies and other insects. In the fastest of water, where the steely ripples cloak its movements, the trout may lie unseen, its presence unsuspected by many who come to seek it with fly, spinner, or worm.

The trout is possibly one of the easiest of fish to recognise. Its back is generally greenish-coloured, but may be a shade of brown, or even almost black. In the clearest of streams it is usually of a pale colour; but trout of the peat-stained mountain streams are usually much darker. All trout have characteristic gold or silver flanks, liberally dotted with red spots. A small adipose fin, which is not found on coarse fish, makes identification easy.

It is a lithe, swift-moving fish that takes bait or fly in a characteristically quick manner, so a keen eye and quick reactions are often needed to hook it. During periods of low water, it often lies where the current is most turbulent. It is easily alarmed by heavy footfalls, or by shadows falling across the water, and once it has been scared it is rarely caught.

The size attained by the trout of small rivers and streams varies considerably. In the barren mountain stream it is usually very small, but in the richer waters of the lowlands it may attain a weight of 5lb or more. Trout of even greater weight are sometimes caught, but they are usually fish which have found their way into the stream from a large river or lake. In such waters trout weighing 10lb or more are occasionally caught.

ANGLING METHODS

The methods used to catch trout are usually dictated by local regulations and preferences. Many anglers never fish for trout with anything but the artificial fly, and on some waters no other method is permitted and even fly-fishing may be restricted to dry-fly as distinct from the sunken-fly. On others, both fly-fishing and spinning are allowed, and there are also waters on which all legitimate methods are permitted. Each angler should acquaint himself with the rules which apply to the water he is fishing; and if the rules stipulate fly only, that rule must be strictly observed. It has not been made without reason, but to give the trout a fair chance of survival. Stocks may be limited, and if all methods were permitted irreversible damage might be done.

FLY-FISHING

Dry-Fly Fishing: Tackle and Methods

Fly-fishing is perhaps the most sporting, and the most fascinating method of catching trout. For the keen fly-fisher there can be few greater joys than to be on the banks of a trout stream in the evening when the flies are spinning gauzily over the water, and the glides are dotted with the delicate rings of rising trout. It is also one of the best times to catch trout with the fly—especially when the water is low and the sun bright. Often one can fish all through a hot summer afternoon without catching a single trout, and then in the evening catch several within the space of an hour, or even less.

The outfit for use on streams should not be heavy or unwieldy. A light, resilient, tip-actioned rod, 7–8ft long, and a fly-reel holding a No 3 (HDH letter code) double-taper line, is ideal—although each angler may, of course, have his own individual preference for both rod and line.

The cast, or leader—as it is sometimes called—should be about the same length as the rod, and tapered down to a minimum of 3lb breaking-strain. It is risky to fish with a finer point than this unless the trout are very small.

A selection of both wet and dry flies should be carried. The dry flies are usually winged, or tied with more hackles than the wet flies, whereas the wet flies are usually only sparsely hackled, as they are required to sink quickly to reach trout feeding beneath the surface.

The actual pattern of fly used is dictated largely by local preference, and by the natural flies that are indigenous to the stream. The angler should learn to recognise the most common types of fly, and should acquaint himself with the artificial pattern that is the closest imitation of that fly.

The subject of fly recognition has been dealt with in several excellent books, and it will suffice here to list a few of the most common flies, and the artificial that is generally used to represent them. The March Brown appears first on many streams, and is represented by an artificial of the same name. The Olives, which include the Large Dark Olive and the Medium Olive, are another species of fly commonly encountered, and are represented by the Greenwell's Glory and Blue Dun. Then there is the Blue Winged Olive, which is represented by the Pheasant Tail. On many streams the little Iron Blue also appears, and is represented by an artificial of the same name. The Mayfly sometimes appears on some streams too—usually in May or June.

This list is by no means complete, but it does form a basis upon which any angler can begin fly-fishing with confidence. Later, he may graduate to the fascinating business of fly-tying, and of attempting to imitate the fly in all its stages of development from a nymph, through to the dun, and finally, to the emergent fly. There will undoubtedly be times when the ability to produce an imitation of the natural fly will be more than useful; but it is also true that exact imitation alone will not catch the fish. In most cases the manner in which the fly is presented, and to a lesser extent, its size, will be far more important.

When the water is low and clear the most delicate presentation is often necessary, and this is best achieved by using the light outfit recommended and a small fly which will fall on to the water like thistledown. The larger fly, fished on a large hook and a strong cast, will not lure many trout in these conditions. When the water is high and coloured, and the sky overcast, a larger fly can often be used; but in the smallest and clearest of streams, where the trout are seldom large, the small fly will invariably lure far more trout.

Dry-fly fishing is traditionally done upstream; but there are occasions when, for various reasons, it is either not possible or not desirable to fish upstream. If so, a downstream cast can be used, provided that the fly can be cast, or drifted, to the rising trout without scaring it. The angler should always try to conceal himself, as far as possible, casting the line loosely so that it allows the fly to travel downstream without drag. Ideally, the fly should alight on the water a yard or so upstream of the rise, and in line with it. The line or cast should never fall across the rise.

Dapping

On many overgrown streams orthodox casting is severely restricted by the conditions; and if this is the case, other tactics must be used. One of the most effective methods is an under the rod-tip style, which is ideal for beginners because no casting skill is needed. It is not even necessary to use a fly-rod. A light, resilient rod, such as the Mark IV Avon, and a fixed-spool reel loaded with line of at least 4lb breaking-strain, will be found just as efficient. The fly itself is tied on to the end of the line in the usual way.

The two most common methods of presenting the fly are simple, but effective. One is designed to imitate the action of a fly that has fallen on to the water, and is struggling to lift off again. In these circumstances the fly vibrates, and whirls round and round on the surface. It is not possible to imitate the rapid vibrations of the fly's wings, but the erratic movements can be imitated by moving the rod-tip from side to side.

The other method is designed to imitate a fly engaged in egg-laying. Flies observed doing this display a characteristic up and down movement. The fly alights on the water, pauses for a few

47

seconds, and then lifts off again, the whole sequence of movements being repeated at intervals. This action is imitated by lowering the artificial on to the surface, and then lifting it off again by raising the rod-tip. Almost any kind of fly can be used, as long as it is well-hackled. In the tiny mountain streams it is better to use a small fly, such as a Greenwell's Glory or a Coch-y-Bondhu; but in the larger, more placid streams, where the trout are bigger, a large Sedge-Fly is a most effective lure.

If the trout respond to these tactics at all they usually do so explosively. Do not strike hurriedly, though. Allow the trout to turn down with the fly first. Stealth and concealment are essential, so never tread close to the edge of the bank, or attempt to peer down into the water—unless this can be done from a safe hiding-place. Only the tip of the rod should appear over the water, and the angler should preferably position himself so that he is downstream of the trout and so less likely to be detected.

These methods of fishing the dry fly need not be confined to those times when the trout can actually be seen rising, but obviously, the angler's chances must be higher when the trout are rising to take flies from the surface.

Wet-Fly Fishing

In the early part of the season, when the water is relatively free of weeds and trout are often disinclined to rise, the wet fly is often more killing than the dry fly. The same outfit as for dry-fly fishing can be used, but I prefer to use a shorter cast—as little as 6ft long. Most wet-fly fishing is done upstream in these small streams, and I find I can achieve a greater degree of casting accuracy by using the short cast.

Some anglers use two or more wet flies, but I prefer only one cast upstream on a short line. I can see little point in attempting long casts in these overgrown waters, and quite often this kind of close-range fishing permits the angler actually to see the trout curving up from its hiding place to seize the fly.

In rough, broken water, it is rarely possible to see the trout, and the 'take' will be indicated by a sudden check in the downstream movement of the line, or a sharp pull that can be detected

Page 49   A stretch of the river Bann, near Hilltown, Co Down. A typical trout stream in its upper reaches with alternating stretches of fast, broken water and deeper pools and flats, it broadens and deepens lower downstream and holds many coarse fish.

Page 50 Fishing a small lowland river while in spate. Fish can often be taken from water only a few inches deep, if the angler makes a concealed approach

with the fingers. The fly must sink quickly, and should therefore be sparsely hackled and well dampened before use. And because of the pace of the current, it cannot be allowed to remain in the water long but most be withdrawn quickly and re-cast, the length of the cast being advanced a little each time until the swim has been covered.

Each little run, glide and counter-current should be regarded as a possible hiding-place, and the fly should be cast into each in turn. No swim should be overlooked—no matter how small and insignificant it may seem—especially where the water is fast-moving. Swims of this type often hold the most trout, and sometimes the biggest, too.

One day, while fishing up a tributary of the Colebrook River, in County Fermanagh, I caught thirty-seven trout on a single wet fly fished upstream; and most of these were taken from swims only a few inches deep, where the water foamed and bubbled in between submerged rocks. Flies with a hint of gold or silver on their bodies, such as a Silver Butcher, Bloody Butcher or Peter Ross, are often very successful in fast-moving water. If the fly does not sink quickly enough a little fine wire should be wound around its body: the extra weight may sometimes make all the difference.

The smoother, more placid glides demand a different technique, for in this type of water the fly must be given added life. The cast is directed upstream and the fly retrieved in a series of little jerks, which are intended to imitate the swimming movements of a nymph, which is the earlier, larval stage of the natural fly. Another method is to recover the fly in a rapid darting manner in the hope of deceiving a trout into thinking it is a small fish. These tactics do not succeed all the time, but they do succeed often enough to make them worth trying. The trout is stimulated into activity by the movement of the fly, strikes, and is hooked. It may seem improbable that such a flimsy creation of metal, feathers and tinsel could be mistaken for a living organism, but fish, fortunately for the angler, are activated by instinct, and the trout is provoked by the movement of the fly.

Downstream fishing with a wet fly can also be a killing method in swims where the water is swift and the bottom clean. Ideally, the fly should be cast up and across, and then allowed to fall back downstream. At this stage the current will push the floating part of the line on ahead of the fly, unless it is mended by flicking it back upstream. The fly must be well sunken. Then, when it has drifted downstream almost to the limit of the cast, it should be checked to bring it curving up to the surface; and it is usually at this stage that most of the 'takes' occur. The line is seen to suffer a brief check, or pull. The strike should then be made in an upstream direction, and in line with the water—not in a vertical direction, or the trout will be missed owing to the sheer weight of line that has to be picked up from the water.

This method of fishing is most likely to be successful in the larger swims, but can be used in the smaller, confined swims too, provided that care is exercised in approaching the swim and in manipulating the tackle. The risk of being detected is not as great in these fast, broken swims, but it is always wise to stay concealed.

Low-water and bright sunshine are not serious handicaps to this method of fishing, nor is there the same need for delicate presentation as in dry-fly fishing. The wet fly does its work *under* the water, and it is how it acts there that is important. Try always to impart some imitative movement to the fly, rather than allow it to drift lifelessly back downstream. Fast water will serve to give the fly some semblance of life, but in the slower moving swims the angler must do this himself by moving the rod-tip and gathering in line.

SPINNING

Of all the methods of trout fishing this is probably the most contentious; and yet, in skilled hands, one of the most effective and most selective methods of catching trout from small, clear streams. It is also, apart perhaps from upstream worming, the method most likely to lure the big cannibal trout from its lair. During the early part of the season, when the weed growth is sparse, I occasionally use a spinner, and with it I have caught some of my very best trout from this type of water. In one day's spinning on a small stream, from which my previous best trout was a 1lb fish, caught on a fly, I caught three big trout weighing 3lb 2oz, 2lb 4oz, and 2lb 8oz.

Many anglers to whom fly-fishing represents the ultimate art object to spinning because of its apparent easiness and its lethal effect. In fact, it is by no means always successful and calls for some degree of skill if it is to yield results. And when weather and water conditions prohibit the use of the fly, spinning becomes the most natural alternative. It should not, however, be practised where other anglers are fly-fishing, for this would be the worst possible breach of angling etiquette.

The tackle required for spinning is quite simple to assemble—provided the basic rule of matching line with rod is adhered to. A light 8½ft spinning rod, a fixed-spool reel, and a reasonably strong line, are all that is required. Spinning should never be done with a weak line, for to risk breakage and to leave a fish with a spinner embedded in its mouth is to commit one of the greatest sins in angling. Minimum strength of the line should be at least 4lb. I often use 6lb, and in those few streams where really big trout are known to exist an even stronger line should be used. Even a moderate two-pounder can put up a terrific fight; and in most streams snags, in the form of tree-roots and weed-beds, are never far away.

The spinner itself should not be too large, since it will be used most often in relatively shallow water. A 1in Mepps spoon is an ideal size, and though the colour may not be of any great significance I favour a gold-coloured spoon, and have caught innumerable trout with it. Possibly its similarity to the natural gold colour of the small trout, upon which the big cannibals often feed, may account to some extent for its deadliness. Fly-spoons, though smaller, are also useful lures to have in reserve. Most of these have a swivel attached, but it is still necessary to squeeze on an anti-kink lead above the swivel, an inch or two up the line. This will help to prevent line-twist and kinking.

Most of my spinning is done by casting *upstream*, rather than down, and mainly in waters too overgrown for orthodox fly fishing. In many cases the spinner must be cast upstream under gloomy overhangs of encroaching vegetation, where the water runs as dark and smooth as silk, and the trout betrays its presence by a sudden swirl, or a sharp furrow across the surface. In this kind of fishing, knowledge of the trout's favourite lies are invaluable, and fast water should always receive special attention.

A good practice is always to fish the nearest water first, casting the spinner up and across the far bank, and then retrieving it rapidly but allowing it to sink a little in the centre of the stream where the water is often deeper. The next cast is advanced a yard or so each time until the final cast is made directly upstream (Fig 2). By doing this one has a chance of picking up trout lying on the back end of the swim first; whereas if the first cast is made directly up into the top of the swim, those trout which are lying further downstream are likely to be scared by the line passing over them. When spinning very shallow water the spinner should not be allowed to sink far, or it will almost certainly get caught up on the bottom, or on a snag. The retrieve must be started as soon as the spinner hits the water. If the trout sees it, it will hit at terrific speed and it will not be necessary to strike.

Many anglers avoid the fast shallow water, but this type of swim is often the most likely to produce trout and should never be missed. A slightly heavier spinner can be used but the method of casting and retrieving should remain basically the same, as long as the spinner is retrieved at a faster rate in order to overcome the speed of the current. In this type of swim, a reel with a high gear ratio is invaluable.

When fishing heavily-weeded swims the spinner should be cast up in between the weeds; or, if they are submerged, spun rapidly over the top of them. Special weedless spinners can be obtained which are ideal for this type of swim.

Success with the spinner can be heady but is by no means automatic. Sometimes, one may fish several miles of rough stream and catch only a few trout, while on another occasion the same stream may produce a dozen or more. With success on this scale, catching trout becomes almost too easy and, having set myself a limit, I then put spinning aside in favour of other more enjoyable and perhaps more challenging methods.

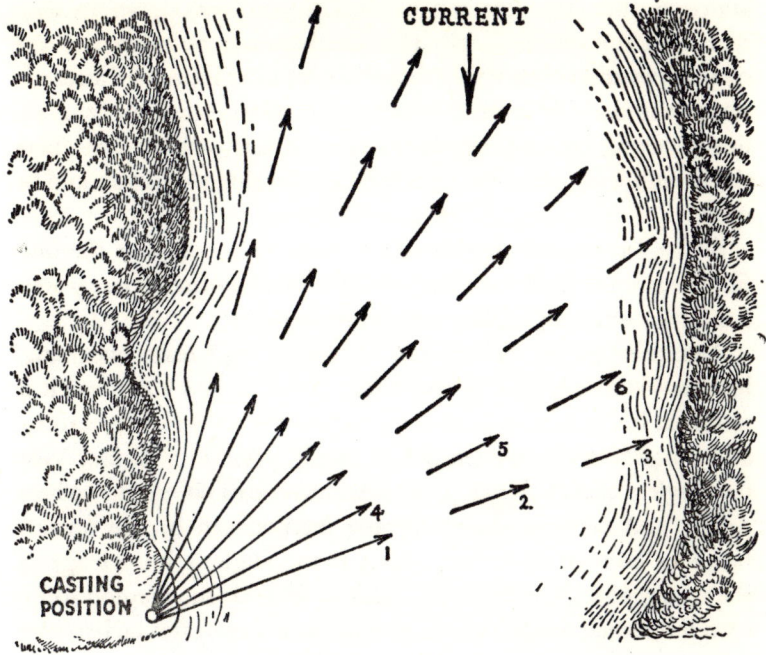

Fig 2 *Suggested casting procedure for spinning upstream so that the swim is covered systematically with gradually lengthening casts*

UPSTREAM WORMING

Upstream worming and rough-stream fishing are so well-suited to each other that one wonders why so few anglers make use of this method. Some anglers, considering it unsporting, profess distaste for it but the art of the upstream wormer is, in fact, in many ways comparable to that of the fly-fisher. The worm is cast lightly and delicately upstream, just as the fly is. There is the same need for accuracy, for stealth in approach, for the observant eye, and for the quick reaction. There is no method of trout fishing that I love better.

The basic needs can be met with a light, powerful, but flexible rod, a fixed-spool reel, and a selection of hooks. The Mark IV Avon is excellent for this purpose, but my favourite is a 9ft sea-trout rod. The line can be of a lower breaking-strain than that used for spinning, but should obviously be related to the conditions and to the size of the trout. In clear mountain streams, where the dark little trout lurk in tiny, effervescent pools, a 2lb line is strong enough, but in the more overgrown waters where the trout are bigger a line of at least 4lb breaking-strain should be used.

Sharp, bronze-coloured hooks in sizes 12–6 complete the outfit. The smaller hooks are used to fish a small worm in clear water: the larger ones for fishing the bigger lobworm.

The method of fishing—as the term 'upstream worming' implies—is simply to cast the worm upstream. As a method it is not new. It was used at least as far back as the seventeenth century, and possibly much earlier; it has simply fallen into disuse. Very few anglers use it habitually, but once anyone has been shown how deadly and yet how enjoyable the method can be, he quickly becomes converted. As always, it is the angler's knowledge of the water, and the manner in which he moulds the method to his own individual needs, that determines whether or not he becomes expert at the art.

The same casting proceedure advised for upstream spinning should be closely followed; but because of the smallness of the hook it is possible to explore many places that could not be fished with a spinner. No swim should ever be rejected as impossible, and as long as there is space to wield the rod a cast is worth attempting.

Fast-flowing, rocky swims, as well as weedy swims, can be explored thoroughly with the worm, just as they can with the fly. The worm is dropped with accuracy into the little boils between and behind the rocks, and in between the weed-beds. In the overgrown places, where the overhanging vegetation meets to form a tunnel, the worm can be flicked upstream with a deft movement of the arm. Fast, broken water, where the upstream worm is most deadly, can be fished with ease. A little weight is sometimes necessary to sink the worm, but this should be used sparingly as the aim must always be to keep the worm in motion—not to sink it to the bed of the stream.

Once the worm has alighted on the water the line should be retrieved at just sufficient speed to keep a little slack line between rod-tip and water. The line should never be allowed to become taut, or the trout will feel the resistance from the rod-tip and promptly eject the worm. When the 'take' comes, the line tightens in an unmistakable manner and the bite should be struck promptly with a sharp but not violent movement of the rod.

This is an all-action method of fishing, and an intensely absorbing one, too, for the endless variations of swim and contour in the stream make every cast a challenge. In time, with practice, the physical act of casting can become almost automatic, and the mind is free to concentrate on the individual problems of each swim.

When fishing up a good trout stream, such as one might find in many parts of Ireland or Scotland, I have often taken double-figure catches of trout on the upstream worm, and on one memorable occasion caught seventy-eight in a single day. Usually, I take away only the largest trout, or just a few for the table, and return the rest of my catch, well content with the enjoyment I have had from catching them and from overcoming the difficulties presented by each swim.

Upstream worming is a deadly method when the water is low and clear, but the best time of all is probably when the water is falling and clearing after a spate. At such times, when the air is sweet and clean after the rain and the little mountain streams wind like a scarf around the cheek of the mountain, I know of no more enjoyable method or one which brings such rich rewards.

TACTICS FOR THE SPECIMENS

Most of the really large trout, weighing over 3lb, I have caught from streams have fallen to either a spinner or a lobworm; and the majority have been taken from streams that run into larger rivers, or into lakes. In Ireland, especially, there are many streams which run into loughs renowned for their large trout, and when fishing up these streams there is always a chance of hooking one of these monsters.

As most of them are cannibals, one of the best baits for them is a small trout, but since most anglers would rightly shrink from such sacrilege the sprat, mounted on a spinning flight or wobbled, is probably the best alternative. Another deadly lure is the big gold or silver spoon, and more big trout are caught with this than with most others—possibly because its movement is suggestive of a darting fish. In most small streams, the big trout will not normally be far away from cover. Like the pike, they prefer to lie in a concealed place—beneath an overhanging tree, bush, or tussock; or beneath a patch of weed—and the spinner should always be worked as close as possible to these hiding-places.

The other killing bait for large trout is undoubtedly the lob-worm, either fished upstream as already described, or legered in some deep hole. I prefer to fish the worm upstream, but there is no doubt that the legered worm will often lure a big trout which may not be inclined to snap at the worm when it appears only briefly in its swim. Occasionally, too, they will fall to a large, bushy fly, carefully cast or dapped close to where they are lying. Even if the trout does not take the fly—and **quite** often it will not—these tactics at least enable you to pin-point its hiding-place, and they seldom move far away. On one occasion, while dapping with a large sedge-fly in a small pool beneath a hawthorn tree, I rose a large trout which, unfortunately, turned down again just when it seemed about to take. A week later I returned to that stream, cast a spinner up under the tree and immediately hooked a 3½lb trout, the largest I had ever caught from that stream.

For the really big loch trout, the time to catch them is when they begin to run up into the streams to spawn, usually from late July onwards, and preferably when the stream is in spate. September and October are generally the best months.

7

Angling for Chub

THE NATURE OF THE FISH

THE CHUB is found in many large rivers, but seems to belong most fittingly to the small river and overgrown stream. Here it finds an environment in which, somehow, it seems to merge. It lurks unseen in deep, shadowed pools beneath ancient willows, beneath 'mats' of debris, thick beds of weed, and overhangs of bushes or grass. It lurks, too, in unseen crevices and recesses, which the floods have carved out in the clay banks; and in the early part of the season, when the sun is full on the water, it may also be found in the fast, oxygenated water of weir-pools and waterfalls.

It is, by reputation, a shy and wary fish, yet sometimes it seems to abandon all its native wariness and feeds with what seems to be almost suicidal abandon. But such experiences can be misleading, and are by no means typical of the chub. For the most part it lies unseen in its chosen haunt, alert to the slightest sound or the merest shadow. If disturbed when it is out in open water it will fade quietly away into its hiding-place, where it will remain for a long, long time. One minute there may be several chub drifting idly to and fro in the current. The next, there is nothing; they vanish so quietly, and so quickly, that sometimes one wonders whether they had ever been there at all.

Some anglers are scornful about the fighting powers of the chub, which, they say, are inferior to those of the trout. This is to some extent true, but it is a limited standard by which to judge any fish. When hooked close to its hiding-place the sheer brute strength of the chub can be a revelation, and even experienced anglers, equipped with strong tackle, are sometimes broken. Beginners often have their tackle broken with what seems to be almost contemptuous ease.

The chub is a strong fish: thick-backed, muscular, and in the depths of winter when it is in peak condition full of power. But the great fascination of the fish is not related only to its strength, but rather to the challenge it offers to the seeker of big fish in small waters. All chub, but especially really big chub, sometimes seem almost uncatchable and will refuse whatever kind of bait is offered to them. They can be seen, and may even allow the angler to get within casting range of them, but they will not take his bait. All chub also have the ability to efface themselves so completely that the angler, coming for the first time to the stream, might think— quite mistakenly—that there are few if any chub in it.

The characteristic appearance of the chub makes it easy to recognise. Generally, its back is greenish-brown; its flanks dull silver or bronze. In some rivers it is more silvery than in others, but very rarely is the silver as bright as on a roach or rudd, with which it is sometimes confused. The fins are a dull, neutral colour, with the exception of the belly fins which are sometimes pink or coral. Its size, and its characteristic blunt head and thick back, make it easy to distinguish from the dace, which it resembles. One means by which it can be identified—even when it is very small—is by the shape of its dorsal and anal fins. Both are *convex*, while those of the dace are *concave*.

The food of the chub varies according to the availability in its environment of the various organisms upon which it feeds. In some waters it is mainly a weed-eater, but it is essentially an omnivorous fish that will feed upon almost anything that is easily available. Caddis-grubs, molluscs, nymphs of all kinds, insects, and other fish, such as minnows, bullheads, loach and elvers, are all consumed by the chub. In some waters it probably feeds more on small fish than it does in others, but there are few waters from which chub cannot be caught with a live minnow or a worm.

The wide range of foods it consumes might seem to indicate that it can be caught quite easily with anything; but it is not sufficient merely to put a bait on the hook and hope that some unwary chub will take it. We can fish with greater expectation of success if the bait is related to an observed feeding pattern, or to a known feeding habit. Certain baits are more effective in some streams than in others, and a few are most effective at certain times of the year. There is no such thing as a best bait, in the sense that it is not possible to choose just one which will always lure a chub. There can only be a best bait for a particular occasion, and the observant angler will notice many small signs which help him to narrow down the choice of bait immensely.

FLY-FISHING FOR CHUB

The big lobworm is probably the best all-round bait for chub in any river. But in the early months of the season, when the streamer weed grows lushly on the shallows and the insect life is most prolific, fly-fishing is often the best method to use. In the evenings, and sometimes in the early hours of the morning, chub can often be seen rising to take flies from the surface. At such times it would be foolish to fish with a sunken bait yet, so strong is the influence of habit, that many anglers do ignore such obvious signs of surface feeding. Others ruin their immediate chances by making a noisy approach to the swim; whereas if they had stayed downstream of the rising fish and cast a fly or bait upstream to them, they might have caught a chub at once. Opportunities such as are provided by a natural rise do not occur so frequently that one can ever afford to ignore them.

The choice of fly is a matter deserving of some thought. Tradition decrees that the angler should always use a large bushy fly, and so many angling writers have repeated this advice that it has now become part of angling lore. But it is by no means always true. Granted there are times when the chub will rise readily to a large bushy fly, but there are also many occasions when they can only be taken on the smallest and daintiest of flies.

Observation of the natural fly that is on the water can provide the most valuable clue. If the chub are rising to take sedge-flies, or mayflies, it is reasonable to assume that a large imitation will also be taken, and this is true more often than not. If, on the other hand, the chub are rising to take midges, iron blues, or olives, it is unlikely that the larger flies will be accepted. A Greenwell's Glory, Iron Blue, Pheasant Tail, or Black Gnat, tied on a small hook, is then more likely to lure them.

Conditions also influence the choice of fly. On hot summer days, when the sun is full on the water and the river is low, the small fly, fished on the finest permissible cast, will usually lure far more chub. Possibly this is because the deficiencies of the artificial, tied on a large hook, are more obvious in the fierce glare of the sun, while the shadow cast by the thicker line, or the sheen of the line itself, may also contribute towards the chub's wariness. In the evening, when the light is fading or the sky is overcast, the bigger fly is often taken more readily. I have often gone out at dusk and taken several chub with a big Sedge Fly fished upstream.

The light fly-fishing outfit recommended for trout fishing can also be used for chub, but in difficult, overgrown conditions the outfit must be much stronger. A 9ft rod, a No 5 line, and a cast tapered down from 8 to 4lb breaking-strain is my normal equipment, and though a fly presented on this kind of tackle may sometimes be refused it is better to persist with the stronger tackle rather than risk fishing with a weak cast, or to wait until dusk when the fly is more likely to be accepted on the strong cast. The angler should always fish with tackle in which he has confidence.

Another effective method is the close-range dapping which was described in the previous chapter. Chub can often be caught like this, even on the hottest and brightest of days, provided the angler can fish from a concealed position. Swims that are overhung by trees or bushes are favourite places for chub to lie in wait for any choice tit-bit that might drift down to them. If they are lying deep, close to the bottom, or in some undercut, it is unlikely that this method will tempt them up; but when they can be seen at mid-water level, or close to the surface, if is often possible to tempt at least one of them up with a fly.

If the chub show no interest in the fly a natural insect, such as a beetle, grasshopper, caddis-grub, or live bluebottle, should be tried. The frantic gyrations of these insects will often bring a chub up to the surface. As when trout fishing, the strike should never be hurried, but rather made when the chub has turned down with the insect in its mouth. Strong tackle is essential. Never risk fine lines when using this method—especially where the chub are big—otherwise the chub is liable to break free, and in doing so will probably scare every other chub in the swim.

When chub show no inclination to rise, wet flies should be tried. Flies with a glint of silver on their bodies, such as the Bloody Butcher, Silver Butcher, Peter Ross, or the Polystickle, are all excellent wet flies for chub. Never be afraid to experiment, there are days when almost anything that moves will attract chub, and many of the flies or lures used for reservoir fishing will catch chub, too. The tried and trusted patterns will serve you well, but there are occasions when something new and different is even more effective. Remember that it is the imitative movement of the fly that attracts, rather than its appearance.

MINNOW FISHING

Another deadly bait for early season fishing is the minnow. When chub are feeding on them, these little fish can often be seen leaping frantically from the water; and in the shallow swims the chub itself can sometimes be seen plunging ponderously forward to gulp in the minnows. Whenever you see these obvious signs of feeding activity, there is no need to bother with any other bait.

Minnows are relatively easy to catch; all that is needed is a single maggot, fished on a size 18 hook. The minnows can then be retained in a bait-can and used as required. Another way is to catch the minnows as you require them. To do this you simply tie a small hook to the reel-line, immediately above the weight, bait it with a maggot, and lower the tackle into the water. Once the minnow has been hooked, you transfer it to the larger hook— preferably a size 6. This method relieves one of the necessity of carrying a bait-can.

Of the several possible methods of fishing the minnow, my

favourite is to toss it upstream on a lightly-weighted cast. When the chub can be seen feeding on minnows this method is deadly; but even when they cannot be seen it is still extremely effective if the angler works patiently upstream, tossing the minnow into every swim likely to hold a feeding chub. In the fast water the chub will often take the minnow violently, but in the slower-moving swims it may cruise slowly up to the minnow and suck it in quite slowly. Few fish should be missed.

Those anglers who prefer to use a float should choose one that will just resist the minnow's efforts to pull it under, and will carry sufficient weight to sink the minnow to the required depth. The tackle can then be cast upstream and allowed to drift back; or, if circumstances permit, it can be drifted downstream. This method is best when the bottom is covered with weed because the float prevents the minnow from gaining cover and concealing itself from the chub. It is also useful when it is necessary to drift the minnow long distances downstream. Strong tackle is essential, and I generally use my Mark IV Carp rod, a 6lb line and a size 6 hook.

UPSTREAM FISHING WITH WORM AND OTHER BAITS

Let us suppose that the chub are not feeding on minnows, or, at least, that they cannot be seen feeding. We could still use the minnow, but as an alternative we could try a worm, fished upstream in the manner already described for trout. This, too, can be a most effective method of taking chub when the water is low and, particularly, just after dawn when the chub are still out in open water.

No weight is needed, except in the fast water, as the worm is heavy enough to sink by itself. The chub sees the worm drifting slowly back downstream, is deceived, and rises to gulp it in. This method may seem almost too simple to be as deadly as it can prove, but in fact it relies a great deal for its success upon the way in which the angler uses it. No hiding-place should be overlooked, no matter how small and unimportant it might seem. Sometimes, by using a bed of reeds or a bush as cover, it is possible to creep right up to the chub, and virtually to lower the bait on to its nose.

This style of upstream fishing is best suited to the low-water conditions of early summer, and minnows or worms are by no means the only possible bait. Quite often, a large piece of cheese, paste, flake, or crust, or perhaps even a black slug, or a small frog will be readily taken. When the September mists begin to shroud the fields the black slug is abundant, and is an excellent bait for large chub. But let us not stray too far ahead.

Another bait for the early season when the water is low, and one which is often as deadly as the minnow or worm, is floating crust. This is most effective when the chub are rising, and they can often be induced to do so by feeding loose crusts into the swim. A piece roughly the size of a 10p coin is then attached to a size 4 hook and tossed into the water. No float is needed, as the crust is large enough to pull line from the reel; but it is necessary to stay alert for the first sign of activity on the part of the chub. When it comes it is unmistakable. Splash! The water boils briefly, the crust disappears, and the line draws suddenly taut. When this happens the strike must be made without delay.

Another, more unusual, method of fishing the crust is to toss it *upstream* with a slow, underhand swing of the arm. It alights softly, almost like a kiss on the surface of the water, and begins to drift back. The slack line is gradually taken in to keep in touch, and the crust watched closely. The first cast may be unsuccessful. If so, another cast should be made into another part of the swim, paying special attention to the fast, shallow swims and the clear runs between the weed-beds. These places are much favoured by chub during the early months of the season, and usually contain some fish.

BOTTOM-FISHING FOR WARY CHUB

No one method or bait can be expected to succeed all the time, and the successful chub angler will be one who is able to relate bait and method to an observed feeding pattern, or to the prevailing conditions. But chub, too, can learn from experience, and will often tend to avoid baits upon which they have previously been caught.

Weather and water conditions greatly influence the feeding habits of chub, and as the season moves on they will be seen less and less on the shallows, and the effectiveness of surface-fished baits, such as the fly and crust, will gradually decline. The angler must learn all he can about the feeding habits of chub, and counter any signs of wariness with a change of bait. Cheese or paste, fished upstream as already described, or legered in some well-known chub swim, will often produce some fine fish during the summer and autumn months. In fact, probably more big chub fall to cheese than to any other bait.

Seed-baits, too, can be a useful alternative when the chub become wary of the more commonly used baits, and wheat, malt, or hempseed will often catch fish which have been refusing all other offerings. The method of fishing seed-baits for chub is quite different from those previously described. A 12ft built-cane rod replaces the Mark IV Avon, a 3–4lb line is used instead of the strong line, and a size 10 or 12 hook is preferred to the large hook. And, instead of moving from swim to swim in search of feeding chub, we choose a swim, groundbait it with one of the seed-baits, and then wait for the chub to find the seeds and start feeding.

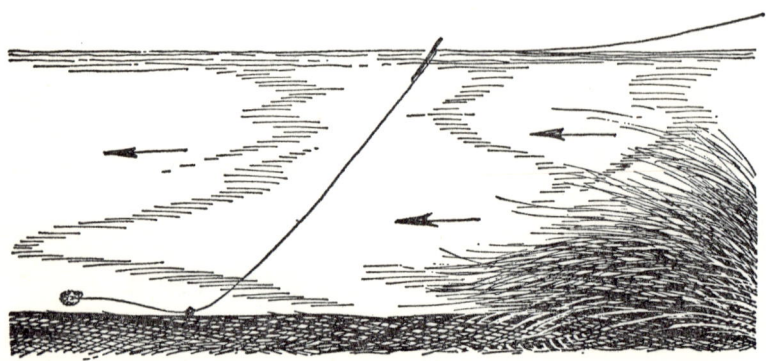

Fig 3   *Float-leger tackle for fishing the bait on the bottom in a downstream direction. A drilled bullet is used as a running leger*

Page 68   (above) *Two big rudd, 1lb 10oz and 2lb 2oz, which were taken with bread flake from a small river; (below) a 4½lb chub which fell to a wheat bait*

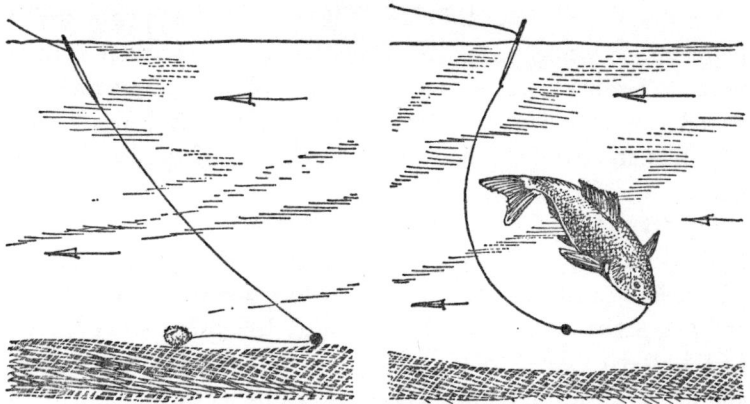

Fig 4   *The same tackle set-up is used as in Fig 3, but the direction of the cast is reversed so that the tackle is fished upstream. When a fish picks up the bait, the float rises and falls back downstream*

This is altogether a more restful style of fishing. A float is threaded on to the line, and the depth adjusted so that the bottom weight will lie on the bed of the swim. The tackle is then cast or lowered into the water and held there—a method which is known as 'laying-on'. Alternatively, in the faster swims, a running leger is threaded on to the line, and stopped from sliding down to the hook by a small weight, or rubber stop (Fig 3).

Both methods are normally fished downstream, but can also be fished upstream, if necessary. If the tackle is cast upstream the float may be pulled under by the current, but will rise to the surface and fall back downstream when a chub picks up the bait, giving an unmistakable indication of a bite (Fig 4). It is a method which can also be used with crust, flake, cheese, or worm, but the seed-baits are more immune to the greedy attacks of minnows, and for this reason alone are often to be preferred for summer-time use.

CHUB IN HIDING

So far we have considered only methods of catching chub that are lying out in open water. But many streams littered with debris also contain numerous overgrown places where chub can hide when the water is low and clear. Whenever this happens—and it happens increasingly as the weeds begin to die off—there is little point in fishing a bait in open water. Instead, the bait must be fished where the chub are hiding—in the undercuts, beneath mats of debris and overhanging trees, in thick beds of weed and in the deepest and fastest water.

For this style of fishing I use my strongest tackle; a Mark IV Carp rod, a 6–8lb line, and a link-type leger tackle. No float is used. The weight is attached to a separate nylon link which has a swivel at its opposite end. The reel-line is threaded through the swivel, and a stop attached to the reel-line to prevent the swivel from sliding down to the hook. The stop can be either a split-shot, a piece of valve rubber, a plastic tube, or another swivel. I prefer the swivel stop and provided it is tied on the line securely, it will not slip, or kink the line (Fig 5).

When using this link-leger method, the angler should work slowly upstream, lowering his bait into every known hiding-place. Sometimes there will be an immediate response. The line draws taut, and the rod-tip bends over in a long, shuddering curve. More often it is necessary to wait and, if so, the bait should be left for several minutes, then inched slowly down the bankside by lifting and lowering the rod-tip. The bait should not be with-

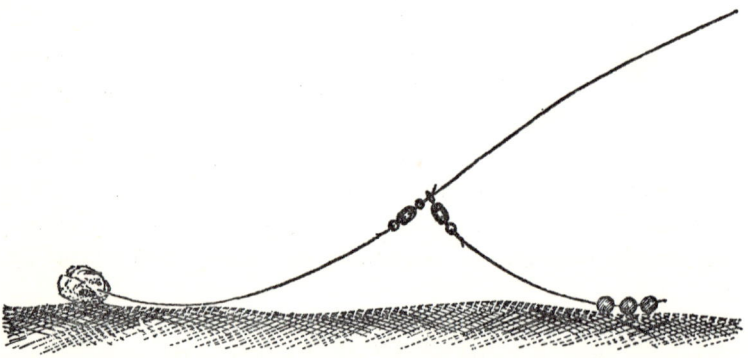

Fig 5 *Leger tackle with one swivel used as a stop and another running loose on the reel-line. Weights are attached to a separate link, which is tied to the running swivel. This tackle set-up is preferable to one which employs a fixed or running weight threaded on to the reel-line*

drawn from the water, and each movement should be performed slowly and carefully. The idea is gradually to cover the entire length of the undercut; but the task should never be hurried, and it may sometimes be advisable to spend an hour or more thoroughly fishing just one undercut.

Weed-beds and mats of debris are fished in a slightly different way. With weed-beds, the tackle is lowered into the clear channels between the weeds, or close to their outer edges, so that the bait will gradually work down under them. Mats of debris are fished by carefully lowering the bait down into the water, close to their upstream edge, so that the current may carry the bait gradually down under the mat. In the slacker swims the bait can be drifted down under the mat, but if the current is strong, a weight must be used to hold the bait away from the debris, otherwise the tackle may get tangled up and lost.

When fishing these kind of places each should be regarded as a challenge, and none dismissed as impossible. If you can get a bait in, and think you have a good chance of extracting any chub you may hook, then try it. Under such conditions the odds favour the chub and some will inevitably be lost; but if strong tackle is used, and pressure applied immediately to pull the chub out from its hiding-place, most of them should be landed.

I recall one such seemingly impossible place formed when a tree, undermined by the floods, fell into the river. In the course of time debris piled up against it, forming a thick mat. To get a bait into a place like this it was necessary to lower it down in between the branches that were above water, and also to avoid those which were submerged. The task was made even more difficult by a strong current which surged between the branches, so that it was necessary to use quite a lot of weight to hold the bait in place. I used an 8lb line to fish this place and even then lost several chub which succeeded in getting under, or in between the submerged branches. None the less, I was able to extract many fat chub before the floods swept the debris away, after which very few were to be seen there.

METHODS FOR SPATE CONDITIONS

A heavy fall of rain can transform the tiniest stream into a torrent of thick brown water. Swims that once contained only a few inches of water now contain several feet, and their character is altered overnight. The angler must adjust his tactics and methods to the new conditions.

While the spate is at its height the big lobworm is undoubtedly the finest bait, and will remain so while the water retains its colour. Chub are more active in the open water, and this can be a great time to catch them—especially when the water begins to fall and clear. The method of casting the worm upstream on a floatless line can still be used, but more weight is needed to counter the increased force of the current. A good big float, such as a swan-quill or goose-quill weighted with several swan-shot, can also be used to fish the slacker water close in to the banks. Areas of calmer water, such as are found in cattle-drinks and the mouths of feeder streams, should be given special attention; they often hold a lot of chub while a spate is at its height.

When the water begins to fall, legering methods are particularly deadly. No float is used. The leger tackle is assembled in the manner described for fishing the undercuts; but it is important to use only just sufficient weight to sink the bait and hold it in position, so that the slightest touch from a chub will dislodge it.

Once the tackle has settled in position, a little slack line should be allowed to form between rod-tip and water. This is important because the first indication of a bite is given when the line begins to tighten. If this indication is missed the bite will be registered on the rod-tip; but it is best to watch the line and to strike as soon as it begins to tighten. Fewer chub will then be missed.

Legering is normally done in a downstream direction, but the upstream style should not be neglected as it is often better to fish upstream rather than down. Indeed, in some swims the upstream method is the only practicable method. Areas of contrary currents immediately below waterfalls and weirs are best fished with the upstream leger. So are bridge tunnels, and those small,

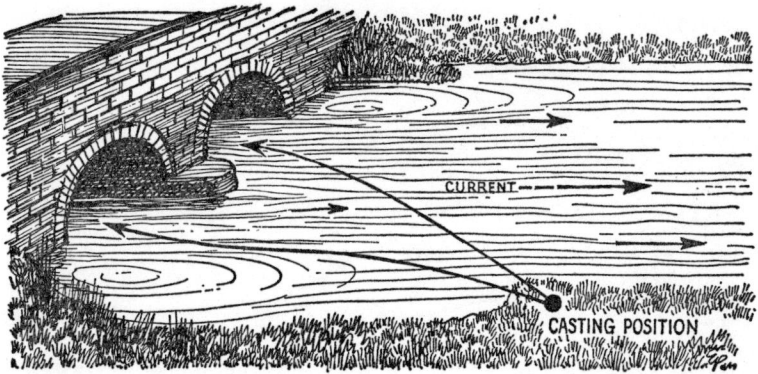

Fig 6 *Fish lying beneath a bridge can often best be reached by upstream legering. The angler is then in a good position to control it when hooked and, aided by the current, to keep his line clear of the sharp edges of the stonework*

confined swims that cannot be fished downstream without the angler placing himself in full view of the fish (Fig 6). It is wise to study each swim, and then decide which method is best suited to it, always remembering that success is more likely if the angler remains undetected. I tend to leger upstream more often than not—unless there is some cover at the upstream end of the swim behind which to hide (Fig 7).

During this period of high water it is sometimes possible to take a large catch of chub from one swim on the leger, the secret of success being to get the chub feeding by groundbaiting at intervals with samples of the hook bait. Once they have started feeding confidently they will often bite for several hours, and large catches are always possible. More often than not, though, it is advisable to move from place to place, taking a chub or two from each swim. Certain swims fish better while the water is high, and it is advisable to concentrate one's efforts on these rather than waste time in unproductive places.

WINTER FISHING

When winter comes and the first frosts begin to whiten the

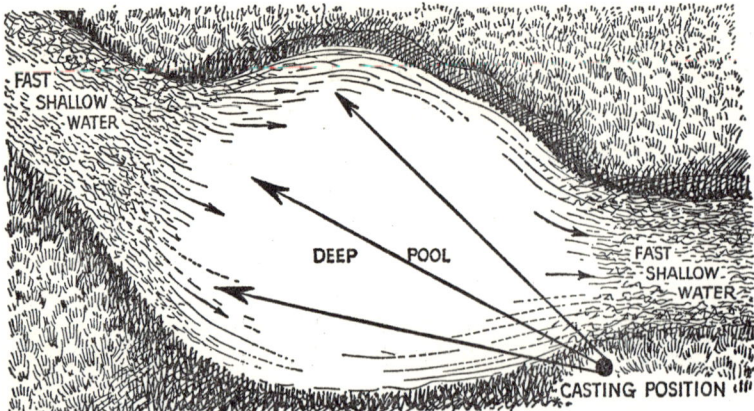

Fig 7 *This typical small pool, lacking cover and bounded at both ends by fast, shallow water, is also best legered upstream as the angler is less likely to be seen and is well situated to play and land his fish*

banks, a marked change occurs in most streams. The leaves fall thickly from the trees, and the weeds gradually die away. The water often becomes glass-clear, and this can be one of the most difficult periods at which to catch chub. During the day, most of the chub will be in hiding and must be sought in their hiding-places if they are to be caught at all. In the evening, when the light begins to fade, they can sometimes be caught out in the open water with a large piece of crust, or flake; but during this difficult period it is best to concentrate on their hiding-places, fishing each in turn until a feeding fish is found. In the course of time one discovers that certain swims will produce chub often, while others will seldom if ever produce a single fish. The deepest swims, close in to undercut banks and preferably situated on a bend in the river, are usually the most productive places. The angler who knows where these places are will often catch chub when others go away fishless.

Once a spate has swept all the leaves away and brought more colour into the water, sport often improves rapidly. At this time of the year I tend to use flake and crust almost exclusively—except during a spate, when I revert once more to the lobworm.

74

SEASON'S END

Towards the end of the season, when all the dead weeds have been swept away, float-fishing methods can be used with much greater chance of success. A 12ft rod, used in conjunction with a 4–5lb line, a quill float, and a size 4 hook baited with a thumb-nail-sized piece of flake or crust, will often produce some splendid catches of chub. It is frequently said that chub prefer smaller baits during the cold winter months, but in my experience this is only sometimes true. Chub do occasionally display a preference for smaller baits, but I tend to use large pieces more often than not, and scale the size of the bait down only if the chub refuse them.

My favourite method is to fish a large piece of flake on a floatless line. This is weighted just sufficiently to sink the flake, which is then cast into the swim and allowed to drift downstream with the current. This method is sometimes referred to as free-lining, or loose-lining, and is especially deadly when the water has fined down after a spate and, when the water is low, during that last hour before dark.

TACTICS FOR THE SPECIMENS

Not all streams hold really big chub, and any chub over 3lb could be classed as a good fish in most streams. In others, chub of this weight are common, and larger fish up to 4, 5, or even 6lb, may also be found—especially if the stream runs into a river that contains large chub. These big chub are not easy to catch, and some anglers fish their whole lives through without catching one.

Most of the chub over 4lb that I have caught from streams have been taken while using the hunting technique, or by legering a bait in some well-known chub swim. They will take a wide variety of baits and success depends mainly upon locating them, and then using a bait which will tempt them at that particular time.

One of the largest chub I ever caught from any stream, weighing a little over 5lb, fell to an enormous piece of flake drifted downstream on a size 1 hook. Another, weighing 4lb 14oz, fell to a lobworm tossed upstream close to a mass of debris. Others have been taken variously with a black slug, minnow, crust, cheese, or a small frog; and a few with either malt or wheat. In those streams where crayfish abound these, too, are an excellent bait.

Particularly do I recall one large chub which lived beneath the roots of an ancient willow, and was in the habit of emerging every few hours to patrol slowly up and down the length of the swim. Provided I remained hidden behind the trunk of the tree, I could watch it through a gap in the branches, and was able to present a bait to it without being seen. On several occasions I tried to catch it with a worm, but as soon as it saw the worm it displayed unmistakable signs of alarm, and I guessed it had been recently hooked on this bait. Crust provoked a similar reaction. Eventually, I caught it after groundbaiting the swim with wheat and allowing the chub to feed undisturbed. I then baited a size 10 hook with a single grain of wheat and lowered the tackle carefully into the swim, just upstream of where the chub was feeding. It was several hours before the chub took the bait, and when it did I struck hard and hauled strongly as the chub was so close to the tree roots that I dared not give it an inch of line. For perhaps about a minute it tested rod and line to the limit; but the 6lb line held and eventually it came to the net. It was a fat, bronze-coloured fish weighing 4½lb. Later, I caught another chub of almost identical weight from the same spot with a small frog dropped into the water close to its head.

In other streams and small rivers, such as the Bedfordshire Ouse, and some of the tributaries of the Hampshire Avon, chub of over 6lb have been caught, but very few anglers ever catch any quantity of them. Perhaps this is because once a large chub has been hooked, it will not usually take that same bait again for a very long time.

Finally, always remember that when seeking large chub, it is essential to keep quiet and never to allow them to see you. Above all, keep trying and make sure that your tackle is strong enough to hold the largest fish you hope to catch—the opportunity may never occur a second time.

8

Angling for Roach

THE NATURE OF THE FISH

THE ROACH is essentially a shoal fish. Very rarely is it seen alone. If you catch one you can be sure that there are others in the swim, though it is unusual to see both large and small fish together. Small roach have different food requirements, and usually move about in separate, larger shoals which, during the early part of the season, can often be seen patrolling slowly up and down a swim. Those who wish to catch them will be well advised to spend some time studying such shoals as a knowledge of their movement patterns will be invaluable when fishing for them.

Roach are easy to identify. They are not big fish. A roach of 3lb or more is an outstanding fish, and very few roach of this size are caught from streams. Roach weighing 2lb or more are not as rare, but are not caught frequently. Below that weight they are found in increasing numbers, and any roach over 1lb is a good fish.

It is altogether a much smaller, slenderer fish than the chub, with which it is sometimes surprisingly confused. Its back is generally bluish-green, its flanks brilliant silver, flushed with a steely-blue sheen. The anal and pelvic fins are coral, the other fins pale brown. The edge of the dorsal fin is concave.

Its tastes in food vary, but it is not a predatory fish like the pike, perch, or chub. Nor is it equipped for pursuit, but rather for gentle browsing amongst the weed-beds, and on the bottom, where it finds the vegetable matter and small organisms upon which it feeds. Its shoaling habits make it essential to fish for it with great care because shoal fish tend to act in unison. Scare one and you scare them all. Within the confines of a small stream alarm is quickly generated; and as the roach flee, panic may spread rapidly to other swims. Once alarmed, the roach is much more difficult to catch.

If, on the other hand, the angler can avoid scaring them and can induce them to feed upon his bait, it is often possible to take quite large catches of them from one swim. A catch of a dozen or so good roach is by no means an uncommon event, and no swim is too small to contain roach.

During the early summer roach are found most frequently where there is a brisk current, and where the weed-beds are thickest. These swims are not easy to fish, but most of them hold fish—especially if they run down into a deeper pool. In such a habitat the roach can find everything for its requirements in the way of food, oxygen, living-space and shelter. In the weed-beds it can find food; and in the fast, oxygenated water a favourable position to lie when the water is low. The pool provides deeper, warmer water, and as the season advances roach tend to fall back from the faster water and are found most frequently in the deepest pools.

Numerous baits can be used to catch roach, but crayfish, minnows, slugs, and small frogs—which are all excellent chub baits—can all be ruled out when fishing for roach. The baits they take most readily are the bread baits, cheese, worms, and the seed-baits. Most of their feeding is done below the surface, so that they are seldom caught with a floating crust. During the early part of the season they do rise occasionally to take flies and other insects from the surface, and when they can be seen doing this both live and artificial flies will often tempt them.

FLY-FISHING FOR ROACH

The flies should be small, and tied on a size 10 or 12 hook. The pattern used is comparatively unimportant, and one afternoon, when I was in an experimental mood, I used no less than seven different patterns of fly and caught roach with each one of them.

It would therefore seem that the manner in which the fly is presented is more important than the pattern used. If they are rising to take flies from the surface a dry fly should be used, whereas if they are taking nymphs from just beneath the surface, or from the bottom, a wet fly or nymph is more likely to be successful.

If there are no specific indications, a wet fly presented on a greased cast so that it hangs just beneath the surface film, is more likely to lure roach than a dry fly. The deeply sunken wet fly should be worked along close to the bottom in a series of little jerky movements in imitation of the swimming movements of a nymph. Provided the roach have not been scared, they will sometimes take a fly presented in this way.

In the evenings, when the sun lays a golden sheen across the water and the air is still, it is a good plan to work slowly upstream, flicking a fly delicately into all those swims known to hold roach. Large catches should not be expected, but this method will sometimes produce a useful number of large roach. During the autumn and winter months roach seldom rise, and fly-fishing methods are not likely to lure many fish.

FLOAT-FISHING WITH SEED-BAITS

Most serious roach fishing is done with baits, and during the warm summer months there is no better bait for roach than one of the seed-baits: malt, wheat, or hempseed. Chub, as we have seen, will also take these baits, but if the seed is fished in a swim known to contain a shoal of roach, it is probably one of the most selective baits that can be used. Malt and wheat are the two I use most frequently; both are larger than hempseed, and less expensive.

The first essential is to encourage the roach to feed on the seeds, because this is not a food they are accustomed to finding naturally in the stream. A good method is to locate a shoal of roach and then feed the seeds carefully into the swim. They should not be thrown directly into the feeding area where the roach are shoaling, but rather into the head of the swim so that they drift down naturally in the current and fall slowly to the bottom. It is then only necessary to wait for the roach to start feeding on the seeds. If they cannot actually be seen doing so, the tackle should be rigged up, baited with a seed, and lowered carefully into the swim. If the roach are going to start feeding at all a bite should not be too long in coming.

Basically, there are two methods of presenting the seed: in a slow-sinking style, or legered on the bottom. If the slow-sinking style is used the line should not be above 3lb breaking-strain, other than in exceptional circumstances. The suppleness of the line is all-important to the success of this style of fishing, and if a strong line is used the bait might be refused. The float should be small: a 3–4in quill is usually big enough, and this should be shotted down so that only the tip of the float shows above the surface. The depth between the float and the hook is then set so that the bait will remain above the bottom when it has reached maximum fall.

The positioning of the weights is quite important if the tackle is to function properly. Remember, the aim is to get the bait falling down through the water in as natural a manner as possible. If the swim is relatively slow-moving it will not be necessary to use a lot of weight. Two or three small weights will probably be sufficient to sink the float down to its tip, and to sink the bait. These weights should be so placed that the bulk of them are attached close to the float, and the smallest an inch or so from the hook. This last weight ensures that the bite is registered more quickly, and a dust-shot is usually sufficient. When the water is fast-moving and the current strong, the amount of weight will obviously have to be increased or the bait will not get down deep enough. But, even so, the slow-sinking style should still be retained (Fig 8).

When roach can be seen, it is often possible to watch both tackle and fish and to note how each behaves. If there is any obvious fault in the presentation of the bait it can then be corrected. One afternoon, when seeking roach, I fished for more than an hour without reward, and was puzzled until I crept up behind a tree and peered down into the swim. I could then see that the roach

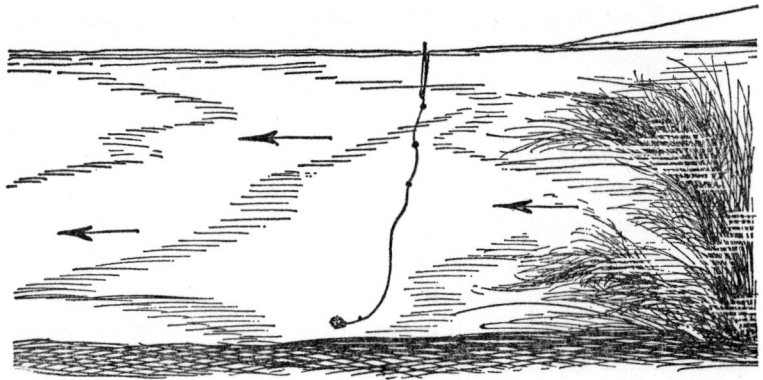

Fig 8 *Tackle set-up for fishing a slow-sinking bait. Note how the weights are spaced so that the smallest is nearest to the hook*

were feeding off the bottom, and that my bait was travelling down the swim just over their heads. As soon as I increased the depth another inch I started to catch fish, and landed fifteen during the next hour. Sometimes failure can be traced directly to the roach not feeding; at others, a little tackle adjustment can make all the difference.

If the roach cannot be seen it is often a wise tactic to start fishing with the bait well off the bottom, and then gradually to increase the depth until bites begin to develop. A few seeds thrown in at intervals will help to establish an off-bottom feeding pattern. A close relationship between the style of fishing used and the pattern of groundbaiting is then established, and good results become much more likely. It could even be said that the angler has it in his power to influence the feeding pattern of roach to a degree he might not have thought possible.

Let us assume, for instance, that the confined nature of the swim makes bottom fishing a more practical proposition, or that the roach are disinclined to move up off the bottom. In these circumstances roach can be encouraged to feed off the bottom by throwing in a larger quantity of seeds than usual, and concentrating them into a small area of the swim. Seed-baits sink rapidly and usually remain where they are put. Once they have settled on the bottom the roach must obviously feed at that depth when they begin to pick them up.

To fish the bait on the bottom the float must be set at a slightly greater depth than the actual depth of the swim, and one weight placed close to the hook. This weight will rest on the bottom and must be carefully chosen to just hold the bait in place. If it is too heavy the roach may detect it and the bites will not develop to a stage where they can be hit confidently (Fig 9).

An alternative method is to use a light, float-leger tackle. A small drilled weight is threaded on to the line in place of the fixed weight. This rests on the bottom, as before, and serves the same function of sinking the bait and holding it in place; but it has the added advantage of allowing the line to be pulled through it, and, theoretically, should lessen the risk of the roach detecting the weight. In actual practice this is not strictly true, and unless the same principle of using only just sufficient weight to hold the bait in place is adhered to the old problem of shy bites is likely to recur. This method can be used in an upstream or downstream style, depending upon which method is best suited to the swim (see Figs 3 and 4). As always, the angler must endeavour to stay concealed, and in many swims he will find it to his advantage to fish upstream.

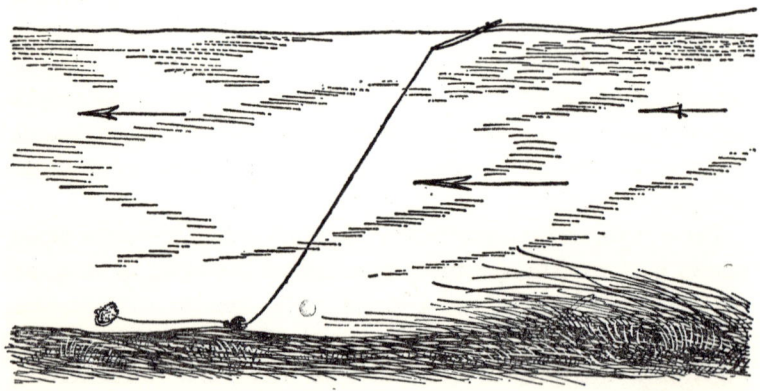

Fig 9   *In this style of fishing the bait is deliberately fished on the bottom. Only one weight is used, and this should just hold the bait in place*

There is, of course, a limit to the number of roach one can fairly expect to catch from any one swim, as the confined nature of many of them makes it difficult to extract the roach without scaring other members of the shoal. It is also possible that the roach may stop feeding, or a pike may move into the swim. It is therefore, wise to bait up several swims, and then to fish each in turn. This will allow each swim a 'rest' period, during which the roach will have time to recover and start feeding again.

Flake, paste, crust, and maggots can all be fished in the manner just described, but during the summer these baits are too attractive to minnows. Cheese is then the best alternative until the onset of the cold weather, or when a spate brings the thick, brown water flooding down.

METHODS FOR SPATE CONDITIONS

During a spate, and for as long as the water remains coloured, the lobworm is unbeatable as a bait for big roach—although a thumb-nail-size piece of crust is a fine bait, too. Chub also feed well on these two baits, but the roach angler can increase his chances by concentrating on those swims where they are known to be most numerous. In the course of acquiring this knowledge certain swims will inevitably become favourites, and the angler should concentrate on these rather than on swims that are not likely to produce many roach.

The obvious places, such as cattle drinks, slack areas of water on the inside of bends, and the mouth of the stream where it runs into a river, should be given special attention; but there may be other swims which hold a lot of roach—especially when the water begins to fall and clear. One of the best small-stream roach swims I can recall was a small pool just downstream of a sharp bend in the stream, and overhung by an ancient willow tree. I usually fished this swim by sitting behind the trunk of the willow and lowering my bait down into the water close in to the bank. The current immediately carried it downstream round the bend into the deeper water of the pool. The response from the roach was often quick and violent, and many fine roach were taken from that swim with a lobworm. It was an ideal swim in many ways, since the willow provided cover, and the bend in the stream ensured that the angler could not be seen by the roach.

Another favourite place in this stream was one where the water ran darkly down a narrow channel between two thick beds of reed-mace. This swim was fished with a lobworm on a floatless tackle, and as the current was very sluggish there was no need to use a weight; the worm was simply drifted downstream between the reeds, and usually one did not have to wait long for a bite.

One of the best catches of roach from this stream was taken one September evening when the water was fining down rapidly after a spate. In this swim a mass of weeds stretched from bank to bank, but in between there were several clear channels into which it was possible to cast or lower a bait. The first cast into this swim produced a real rod-bending bite, which was hit successfully and produced a roach weighing 1lb 4oz. Several minutes elapsed before the next bite, and when it came another fine roach weighing 1lb 6oz was hooked and landed. To encourage the roach to keep feeding, the swim was then baited with broken worms and although some bites were missed, by dusk I had fifteen beautiful roach in the keep-net. The largest weighed 1lb 8oz, and none were less than 12oz—all magnificent fish for such a little stream.

The method used to fish this swim was the link-leger tackle recommended for chub (see Fig 5). The line was of 4lb breaking-strain, the hook size 6, and the tackle was weighted with one split-shot. The rod was a Mark IV Avon, and no float was used.

When legering for roach it is noticeable that they do not usually take the bait as wholeheartedly as chub do, and are much more likely to drop it if they feel any unnatural resistance. Great care should therefore be taken to get the presentation just right. Use only enough weight to sink the bait slowly to the bottom, and use a rod that has a flexible tip, at least. And always leave a little slack line from rod-tip to water. This will allow the roach to pick up the bait and move several inches before it begins to feel any resistance from the rod-tip. Upstream legering is, of course, the best answer to shy, difficult-to-hit bites.

TACKLE FOR LEGERING IN LOW, CLEAR WATER

Even when legering, there are times when it is advisable to use a lighter and finer tackle to overcome the problems caused by low, clear water and bright sunshine. In these circumstances a finer line will often give a more natural action to the bait, but it is not sufficient merely to scale down the strength of the line. The reduction in line strength must be matched by using a rod of greater flexibility. I use a 9ft wet-fly rod which, though flexible, is rather stiff-actioned. With this rod much finer lines can be safely used, and this tackle, and a smaller hook, will catch roach where the stronger tackle would have failed.

WINTER FISHING

When the first winter winds begin to blow keenly across the meadows, stripping the leaves from the trees and bringing the first flurries of snow, bread-baits come more and more into their own. In the depths of winter I use little else—except during a spate, when I switch once more to lobworm and crust. Undoubtedly the best bait for roach fishing in the low clear water that is so often encountered during the winter is bread-flake.

In these conditions a line of around 2lb breaking-strain, a tiny quill float, and a size 10 or 12 hook baited with a small pinch of bread-flake, is almost standard tackle for fishing the bait in a slow-sinking style. The faster water can be fished with either a light leger tackle, or by laying the bait on the bottom and using a float as previously described.

In many streams and small rivers the cold winter months provide the best of roach fishing. Not all days are good days, of course; but even when the banks are white with snow there is no need to give up hope. Many of the best catches of roach have been taken in sub-zero temperatures.

The feeding period may be of limited duration, and occurs

F

most frequently during the afternoon or evening, though sometimes feeding may not start until the last hour of daylight. I can
remember fishing the willow tree swim on three separate occasions one winter afternoon. The first two occasions produced
nothing, but on the third the roach began feeding madly, and
sixteen of them up to 1lb 5oz were caught, all on bread-paste
rolled downstream on a size 6 hook tied to a 6lb breaking-strain
line. Fine tackle could not safely be used in this swim, and as the
bait was being fished on the bottom the roach were not put off
at all by the thick line.

Roach can be encouraged to start feeding by careful groundbaiting, but it should be used sparingly in cold, winter conditions.
Mention must also be made of maggots and chrysalids, both of
which can be used to catch roach during the winter, provided
they are presented on a small hook.

TACTICS FOR SPECIMEN ROACH

Theoretically, the task of catching big roach from streams can
be reduced to a few simple rules. First, if possible, find out where
the bigger roach lie. Fish for them at what you find from experience to be the best times. Stay quiet and concealed. Give each
bait a fair trial. Do not give up if success is slow to come and
usually it is. Lastly, do nothing to encourage small roach to feed
in your chosen swim.

Generally speaking, one should not expect to catch a lot of
big roach from the average small stream. Any roach over a pound
in weight is a very good fish by normal standards, and by no
means easy to find in most waters. Roach over 2lb in weight are
even greater rarities and it is an achievement to catch even one
of this size in a season.

The problem of singling out large roach from the small ones
cannot be solved simply by fishing the bait hard on the bottom,
in the mistaken belief that big roach invariably feed there. Big-
stream roach will, in fact, feed at whatever level in the water they
can find the kind of food they want at any particular time. This
means that you might find them feeding upon bottom-living

organisms, taking nymphs from the surface, or intercepting food that is drifting down on the current to them.

What is important is to fish in such a way that small roach are not encouraged to feed in the swim. This means dispensing with fine groundbait and baiting up with the hook bait alone. The best baits for big-stream roach are lobworms, crust, and flake.

Timing is important, too. During the summer, early mornings and evenings are great times for big roach, but during the winter the last hour before dusk is possibly best when the water is low. When it is high and coloured, the best time is often when the water begins to fall and clear.

The first roach of specimen size I ever caught from a stream fell to a lobworm, fished upstream on a weightless and floatless line. It was a fine summer evening, and I had progressed slowly and carefully upstream, casting my bait lightly into every accessible swim. Eventually I arrived at a place where the water ran swiftly down over a bed of gravel, spurting between two long, wavering fronds of weed, and finally washed gently against a high, clay bank.

Standing quietly on the grassy bank where the water from the pool slid smoothly over the shallows, I cast the lobworm lightly up against the clay bank and eased it down into the water. For a second or so nothing happened; then the line tightened slowly in a manner that could have been caused by the bait lodging against an obstacle. I struck and immediately felt the pulsing reaction of a hooked fish. A few minutes later I netted a 2lb 5oz roach, the largest I have ever caught from a stream.

Almost two years elapsed before I caught another roach of comparable size. It was in March, when the water was falling and clearing after a recent spate, and the swim, situated on a bend, was overgrown with willows. It was not easy to fish as the deepest water was immediately beneath the willows, but there were some clear spots into which it was possible to lower a bait. This time I baited with crust on a size 8 hook and lowered the tackle carefully into the tiny space between the branches. Within a second or so the line flickered and tightened. There was no room to play the fish in such a confined swim, so it was struck instantly, hauled quickly to the surface and netted. It was a beautiful fish: fat, perfectly scaled, and brilliantly coloured. I fumbled excitedly for my scales and weighed it. The needle flickered just on the 2lb 2oz mark.

In this case the most important factor was undoubtedly the choice of place. Water conditions and temperature were also favourable and, for the second fish, the crust bait was chosen as a good one for clearing water. In isolation, these things seem comparatively unimportant, but it is upon such seemingly insignificant details that success with specimen roach is built.

9

Angling for Perch

THE NATURE OF THE FISH

THE PERCH, to me, is the most enigmatic fish of the stream. When it is small and on the feed no fish is easier to catch; but as it grows larger so does it become more wary, more difficult to locate, until, when it reaches specimen size—which in a stream is between 2 and 3lb—it may rarely be seen or caught. Smaller perch, up to about 8oz, move about in large shoals which can often be seen, but even perch of this size sometimes display a complete indifference to baits. The most carefully presented minnow or worm will be ignored. In some streams the perch is quite common; in others it may not be found at all. In just a few it may be so numerous that it could be classed as a nuisance. As with all other fish, a higher ratio of success is achieved by fishing specifically for perch rather than for anything that might happen to take the bait.

Not a large fish, and rough to the touch, the characteristic hump-back of the perch makes it impossible to confuse it with any other species. Its back varies in colour from dark green to bottle green, its flanks are a paler shade of green, and its belly milky-white. Six dark bars run vertically down each flank, giving the perch a distinctive, striped appearance. Its large mouth contains slanting teeth, and it has two dorsal fins, both prickly with spikes. The gills are also spiny and can inflict a sharp wound if grasped carelessly. Like all predatory fish it feeds extensively on smaller fish: minnows, loach, bullheads, and the fry of other fish.

It will also eat its own fry. In infancy nymphs and other small organisms form a large part of its diet, but as it grows older it turns increasingly to eating other fish.

Perch are not often found in fast, streamy water—except during the early summer months—and will usually not be far from some deep hole. Swims lined with reed-mace, bulrushes, or over-hanging bushes, are much favoured places; and sometimes, when the water is low, it is possible to see them poised there in the slow currents. Shoals are seldom large, but observations of this nature are invaluable because they enable the angler to fish where he knows there is a good chance of catching perch, and also accurately to locate the larger fish.

Because of the predatory nature of the perch, most baits used for the other species are of little use and the only ones of any significance are small fish, worms and maggots, in that order of preference. Maggots have the disadvantage of not being selective enough, and of attracting too many small fish, but they should be included because there are times when perch prefer them, and they will quite often start off a chain reaction in which min-nows are attracted by the maggots, and perch, in turn, attracted by the small fish.

Worms are most effective during a spate, and for as long as the water remains coloured. They can, of course, be used in any condition of water, but perch seem to prefer them when the water is coloured. Exactly why this should be so is difficult to say, but it is a feature of perch fishing that is worth remembering.

FLY-FISHING

Fly-fishing is one of the least effective methods of catching perch from streams, and fishing a dry fly upstream, which is often used to catch trout and other fish, can be excluded completely. Perch seldom rise to a dry fly in running water, but wet flies of the Butcher type fished downstream are always worth trying during the warm summer months. The flies should be well-sunken and worked back through the swim in a series of rapid jerks to imitate the movements of a darting fish. A nymph, worked slowly across the bottom in a typical swimming motion, will also tempt an occasional perch.

SPINNING

Apart from bait fishing, spinning is one of the most effective methods of catching perch. The spinning outfit already recommended for trout can also be used to spin for perch. The spinner itself should be small—perhaps a fly-spoon, or a 1in gold or silver Mepps spoon—while another deadly lure is the Voblex spinner, which closely resembles a minnow.

A sound method is to fish the spinner upstream, concentrating on all swims likely to hold perch. The spinner should not be allowed to fall below mid-water level, and should then be retrieved in an erratic manner in the hope of deceiving the perch into thinking it is a small fish. The straightforward, fast retrieve is seldom as effective.

Each swim should be fished carefully and thoroughly, no matter how difficult it may seem. Perch often lie close to reed-beds or snags, and the angler who can cast his spinner accurately into the more difficult swims will often catch more perch than one who concentrates only on the cleanest, most accessible swims.

A small dead-bait, such as a minnow, small roach, dace, loach, or rudd, mounted on a spinning flight or on a wire trace and a small treble hook, will often lure perch, too. If a spinning flight is used, the dead-bait will spin as it is retrieved; but the dead-bait mounted on a simple wire trace is more effective because it can be made to act in a variety of ways. It can be wobbled, made to dive, or to dart from side to side, and the more life-like the movement of the bait the more likely is the perch to respond to it.

The chance of success with either of these methods will obviously be greatest when perch can be seen hunting fry. The signs are unmistakable. Fry will be seen leaping frantically from the water, and swirls will be observed close behind them. Sometimes a spiny dorsal fin will also be seen breaking through the surface. Whenever this form of activity is seen the spinner should be cast up amongst the feeding perch and it would be surprising if at least one was not speedily caught.

MINNOW FISHING

One of the advantages of spinning is that it is not necessary to re-bait the hook; but it must be admitted that no lure composed of metal and feathers can be as attractive to perch as the natural fish. So, when perch can be seen hunting minnows the obvious course is to procure some as quickly as possible—by the methods already described on p 63—and use them for bait.

Tackle needs are met with the Mark IV Avon rod, a 4lb breaking-strain line, and a size 6 hook. The minnow is lip-hooked and cast upstream into the feeding shoal, and the response is usually immediate and violent, provided the angler stays down-stream of the shoal. Once the feeding spell is over no more bites can be expected in that swim, and it is best to move on.

Though this method is most effective when perch are hunting minnows, they can often be tempted at other times by casting or lowering the minnow into every likely spot. I usually fish the minnow on a floatless line, but a float can sometimes be useful for holding the minnow up off the bottom, or above weed in which it might hide.

UPSTREAMING THE WORM

An alternative bait to use in conjunction with this method is the worm, and it can be fished in a variety of ways. One way is to flick it upstream in the same manner as advised for trout and chub. A very small weight may be necessary to sink the worm in the deeper, faster-flowing swims, but when fishing the slow-moving swims the worm will sink naturally under its own weight.

Perch are attracted by a bait that moves quickly and, apart from any current there may be, additional life can be given to the worm in several different ways. One way is to retrieve it by reeling in so quickly that the worm spins or undulates attractively through the water. Another way is to retrieve the worm in a series of jerky movements similar to those used to retrieve a wet fly. The cast is normally made upstream, but the method can be used downstream, or even right under the rod-tip when the nature of the swim permits such a close approach.

PLAYING THE WAITING GAME

The methods so far described are designed to catch perch from many different swims. Let us assume, however, that a shoal of perch has been located, and that the angler decides to concentrate on this swim in the hope of catching a quantity of them. For this, he must alter his tactics and patience and persistence now become more important than the ability to make a quick, accurate cast to a feeding perch.

Light legering methods can be used in many swims, and indeed may be best where the water is fast-moving. Perch will pick up a bait off the bottom, but they are not habitual bottom-feeders and are generally best fished for with the bait held up off the bottom. For this reason the link-leger style of fishing is generally to be preferred, with the length of both the trail and the link increased to at least a foot. The weight is then carefully adjusted so that it will carry the bait slowly down to the bottom. Once the bait is in position, a little slack line should be allowed to form between rod-tip and water. The rod itself should then be placed in a rest and the line watched carefully for any sign of a bite. A line of between 3 and 4lb breaking-strain is usually strong enough.

The ideal way to fish with this tackle is to get as close as possible to that part of the swim where the perch are lying, always taking care to remain out of sight. In many swims the perch will be found close under the banks, or close to the edge of the reed-beds, so only the rod-tip should protrude. Either a worm or a minnow can be used as bait.

A float can be used in conjunction with this method as an aid to bite indication, if desired; but it does not need to be large nor is it even necessary that it should actually enter the water. Indeed it is often better to adjust it so that it is *above* the water where it can be more easily seen (Fig 10).

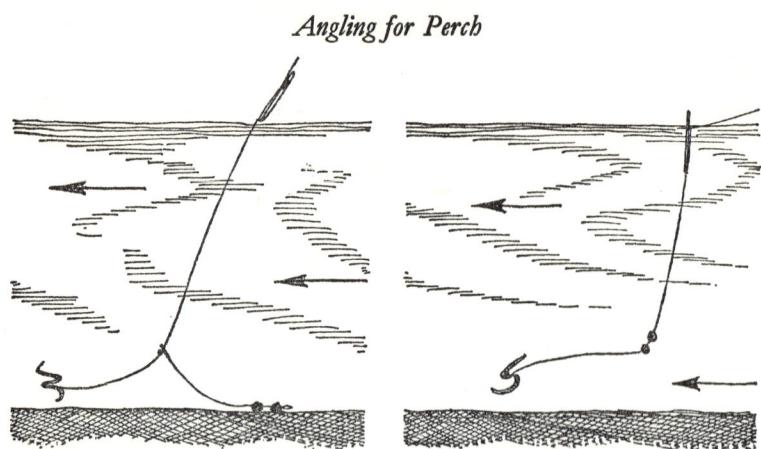

Perch-fishing tackle: (left) Fig 10 *Using a sliding link leger and a float secured* above *water where it acts as a bite-indicator and offers no resistance to the current;* (right) Fig 11 *With the weights concentrated at mid-water level, leaving a long 'tail' of line between weights and bait*

An alternative to fishing with a worm is to use a straight-forward float tackle. The float should be threaded on to the line through both rings and the shot concentrated at mid-water level so that the worm is free to waver enticingly in the current. As with the link-leger method, the tackle should be lowered into the swim and held under the rod-tip. This method functions best in the slower-moving swims, but is also useful for holding the bait up above a weedy bottom (Fig 11).

Emergent, or semi-emergent reeds pose a different problem. In many streams and small rivers there are swims which, in summer, are overgrown with lilies. These swims also often hold some good perch, but the areas of fishable water may be limited to a few small clear spaces between the lilies. Obviously, in these circumstances, a moving bait cannot be used and the tackle must be adjusted so that once the bait has been lowered into the hole it will remain there.

It is possible to fish in between the reeds by using a fixed float tackle, provided a worm is used as bait and the tackle is not left in the hole too long. The procedure is to lower the tackle into a hole, and to allow the worm to sink slowly down through the water. After a few minutes the tackle is withdrawn and another hole tried. This exploratory method of fishing, designed to catch any perch that may be lying between the reed-stems awaiting a choice tit-bit of food, works well enough where there is no appreciable current, but obviously cannot be used where there is a strong current likely to ensnare the tackle around the stems of the lilies. A method which will hold the tackle firmly in position is then required and the link-leger, or paternoster style, is the best answer to this problem (Fig 12).

BEST TIMES

There can be few situations in which one or other of the methods described could not be used, but in the final analysis it is the angler who understands perch, who knows where they can be found, and, even more important, knows *when* to fish for them, who will achieve the greatest measure of success.

In my experience of perch fishing, the best time to seek them is when the river or stream is running a little higher than normal level, especially if the day is mild and the sky overcast. It has

Fig 12   *Tackle for perch fishing in a thick weed-bed, where the bait must be held in one spot continuously. The weight holds the tackle steady, but the running link allows the bait to be taken freely*

been noticeable that bites decrease as the water falls and clears, until, when the water is at a low level and very clear, perch become much more difficult to catch. The worst conditions seem to be low, clear water, and low temperature, so that during the winter, perch are particularly difficult to catch.

Towards the end of the season, when the spring spates bring the streams roaring down bank-high and the weather is suddenly mild again, perch fishing improves and this can be a great time to seek them. The weeds have all gone, the dead leaves and other debris swept away on the swift, brown floods. At this time of the year the barred perch will often bite eagerly, and good catches can be made with either worm, minnow or spinner. But each day is different, as are all angling days, and you may catch a dozen or more on one day and on another seek them in vain in every known swim. Perch fishing in streams is like that.

TACTICS FOR THE SPECIMENS

I once caught a 2½lb perch from a deep hole beneath a tree simply by lowering the worm into the water close in to the bank and allowing it to sink to the roots of the tree. After a minute or so I drew it quickly up towards the surface, and this sudden movement provoked a large perch into making an attack. A dark shape emerged from beneath the roots, snapped at the worm, and hooked itself. Though I fished that spot many times afterwards, hoping for a repeat performance, I never caught another perch there of comparable size. When I did catch another it was from another swim, and in a totally different way.

In this swim a fast current swept down over a long, shallow glide, surging finally into a small but deep pool which was overhung by a stunted hawthorn. The deepest part of the pool lay close to the opposite bank, immediately beneath the hawthorn. Some instinct prompted me to flick the worm up into the fast current so that it would drop slowly back downstream into the deeper water. There was a momentary check in the downstream movement of the line—an almost indiscernible trembling which I interpreted as a bite. I struck, and immediately felt the solid, throbbing pull which is typical of the perch. A few seconds later I caught a brief glimpse of its barred flanks as it turned in the current, and could see that it was big. When finally landed, it proved to weigh 2lb 4oz.

Afterwards I wondered how many long months, or years even, those two perch had lurked deep in their separate hiding-places. How many worms had they seen, how many minnows? And why had they both succumbed to temptation just when they did? In the first case it may be that the rapid movement of the worm provided the necessary stimulus. In the second it may have been sheer good luck to have arrived at that swim just when the perch was looking for food. It is significant though, that in both cases I fished upstream from a concealed position, and that neither of the perch was aware of me.

These larger perch will sometimes fall to a spinner, too, but, as always, the most important thing is to locate them, and this can only be done by patient exploration, or by observation. On occasions when the water is low, they can be seen, but most of the time the big perch is inclined to stay in, or near to its hiding-place, beneath a tree, or under the bank—except when it is actively hunting down its prey. Shallow water can, therefore, usually be disregarded, and the best swims in which to seek the big perch are those in which there is plenty of weed or in the deep pools of the stream.

10

Angling for Dace

THE NATURE OF THE FISH

THE DACE is an ebullient little fish that can be found in most streams and rivers, and although it is equally at home in both shallow and deep water, it is found most frequently in both flowing swims and over a clean bed of gravel.

In appearance it differs in several ways from the small chub, with which it is often confused. It is more silvery, its head is much more sharply pointed, and its dorsal and anal fins are *concave*. Rarely found alone, small shoals of dace can often be seen drifting to and fro in the shallow water close to the surface.

Of all coarse fish, dace are probably the most habitual surface feeders, and will readily rise to sip in nymphs and small flies. They rise most frequently during the summer, but will also do so even in winter if the day is reasonably mild and the air still.

Like roach, dace may share their swim with other species, but move about in quite separate shoals varying in size from about a dozen fish to larger shoals of up to fifty or more. The shoals are thus comparatively easy to locate, but they are also easily scared, and each swim should be approached quietly and with great care.

Dace can be tempted with several different baits, but if we apply the policy of choosing only the most selective baits the choice can be narrowed down to flies, both natural and artificial; chrysalids, and to a lesser degree, floating crust. Chrysalids are perhaps the most selective bait of all and though flies can also be deadly, the confines of a small stream will often preclude their effective presentation.

The method of fishing a worm upstream, so often deadly for other species, will also sometimes catch odd dace, but will seldom yield any quantity of them. More dace can be caught by locating a shoal, and then settling down to fish for them in that one swim.

FLY-FISHING

Let us assume that the angler arrives on the banks of the stream in the evening, when the sun is low in the sky and the glides are dimpled with innumerable splashy rises. The experienced angler will recognise at once that these are caused by dace, and that he now has an excellent chance of catching them with either an artificial fly, or a live one.

The rod he chooses will be light, tip-actioned, and matched with a light line, the finest permissible cast, and the tiniest of flies. The cast will be made upstream, because in the clear waters of a stream it is seldom feasible to use a downstream style. The fly could be a Black Gnat, Pheasant Tail, Blue Dun, or Midge, tied on a size 14 hook. Dace will, on occasions, take quite a large fly, but in general the smaller flies are more killing.

Haphazard methods sometimes succeed, but it is better to fish to some kind of plan, flicking the fly upstream to the nearest rising fish first. If a dace is hooked immediately it should be reeled back quickly out of the swim. The next cast is then advanced a little further to cover the other dace that are rising higher upstream. If this procedure is adopted it is often possible to catch several dace from the same swim, whereas if the first cast is made over the heads of fish lying close to the lower end of the swim, they will be put down, either by the line falling across them or by the struggles of the hooked fish. If the sun is behind the angler it will throw his shadow upstream, and he must overcome this difficulty by making longer casts.

If wet flies or nymphs are used, both the approach and the casting must be done with the same care, but the lures are fished so that they hang just beneath the surface film. To achieve this effect the cast should be lightly greased up to within about half an inch of the lure, and the lure itself thoroughly wetted so that it will sink quickly through the surface film. The cast is then made upstream on a snaky line. The line should never be taut, or the current will quickly exert a strong pull on the line and the action of the fly will appear unnatural to the keen-eyed dace lying just beneath the surface.

As dace are so very easily frightened the angler should always start at the downstream end of the swim and work gradually upstream, concentrating on those swims in which dace can actually be seen rising. Much time and energy can then be saved, as there are swims in most streams, generally deep and slow-moving, in which dace are seldom if ever seen.

The method of retrieving a well-sunken wet fly in a jerky manner as described for trout and chub, can also be used to tempt dace, although it is not usually as effective as the other methods mentioned. Of them all, the dry-fly method is probably the most effective on most occasions, and even when not actually rising dace can sometimes be tempted up with a delicately-cast fly.

The dry-fly method also has the advantage that one can often see the dace rising to take the fly, and so time the strike exactly; whereas with the wet fly the line must be watched closely or the take will be missed.

When the day is stormy and the wind whips keenly across the stream, other methods of dace fishing will be more productive; but first let us look more closely at an alternative method of surface fishing with a live fly or chrysalid.

SURFACE-FISHING WITH CHRYSALIDS

The method is akin to fly-fishing in the sense that the bait is fished on the surface, but in all other respects it is completely different. It is a static rather than a mobile style of fishing, and the bait is mainly fished in a downstream direction. It is, therefore, essential that the angler finds a position from which he can fish without being observed, for if the dace are put down by a careless approach they may not appear again for a long time. A bush, a patch of reeds, some long grass, or even a bend in the river, will suffice, and it is also helpful if the angler keeps low down on the bank. And if one sits on a plastic sheet, instead of a stool or basket, it is possible to catch dace virtually under one's rod-tip.

When dace are rising they will be feeding off either flies or hatching nymphs, but this does not mean that they will not accept chrysalids. If a thin but steady stream of these is kept drifting down the swim the dace will usually start feeding on them sooner or later, for very rarely do dace display any degree of preoccupation with the natural fly. The chrysalids should never be thrown into the swim in large quantities, or the dace will follow them downstream and may move out of the swim altogether. Sufficient chrysalids should be thrown in to keep them interested, but no more.

The tackle needed for this delicate kind of fishing is completely different from that used to fish for most other stream fish. The rod should be at least 11–12ft long, of built-cane or fibreglass throughout, and capable of being used with a line of as low as 1lb breaking-strain. Line of 2lb breaking-strain should be regarded as the strongest line it is normally necessary to use—and then only when the dace are lying in a reedy or snaggy swim. The longer, flexible rod enables one to lower the tackle into the stream and to reach out over intervening reed-beds. A small quill float and a size 16 or 18 hook completes the outfit.

Success with this method depends greatly upon the deceptive presentation of the chrysalid. It must appear in the dace's line of vision as naturally as the free offering does, and this effect is achieved by manipulating the float down the swim so that the line between float and hook is never taut. In the normal course of events the float will travel downstream at a slightly faster rate than the chrysalid, and in the faster-flowing swims may even overtake it. This tendency of the float to overrun the bait can be corrected by checking the float just before it reaches that part of the swim in which the dace are rising. The float can then be released again to allow the chrysalid to drift down over the heads of the rising dace without restraint. The line between float and hook should, of course, be entirely free of any weight.

Bite detection is a simple matter and is signalled by a rise, or by a sharp movement of the float. Since the rise must occur a split second before the float begins to move, it is best to watch for the rise and this can be more clearly discerned if no chrysalids are thrown in at the same time as the tackle is drifted down the swim. Otherwise it becomes extremely difficult to distinguish a rise to the hook-bait from rises to the free offerings. It is better to throw in a few chrysalids first, and then to drift the hook-bait down *after* them.

Another important point is to try always to keep the chrysalids travelling down the same path in the swim. Dace often tend to remain in one position in the swim—usually where they are in the best position to intercept any floating insects the current may bring down to them. If the chrysalids are drifted down this part of the swim they are more likely to be taken than if they were drifted down those parts of the swim where the dace must move many yards to intercept them.

I experienced a convincing demonstration of this one afternoon when a shoal of dace were rising in a shallow swim which was lined with willows along its far bank. The dace were rising close to the willows where the water had its briskest movement, and it was essential to drift the chrysalids down as close to the willows as possible. Any chrysalid that was drifted down the swim close to the near bank remained untouched. The long, 12ft rod I was using enabled me to hold the float out and drift it downstream close to the willows; and by sitting quiet and concealed behind a bed of nettles, I was able to catch twenty-two dace from that swim during the afternoon. This is by no means exceptional by big river standards, but was a creditable catch for a small stream.

If one is not fortunate enough to find dace rising, they can often be encouraged to do so by drifting a stream of chrysalids down over them. Shoal fish are ruled by a common instinct, and once one dace begins to rise the others soon follow suit, until eventually the whole swim may be covered with rises. If this does not happen it is likely that the dace are not interested in taking food from the surface, and the bait must be fished in a style which will allow it to sink down to where they are feeding.

FISHING THE SUNKEN CHRYSALID

Below-surface chrysalid fishing is best done with casters, which will sink gradually under their own weight, or with a floater weighted with a small weight placed close to the hook. A dust-shot will usually be sufficient. The float is then set to allow the bait to remain clear of the bottom when it reaches maximum fall. Now it is no longer a surface-fished bait, but a slow-sinking one which the dace will not have to rise to the surface to find.

When using this style of fishing the chrysalid, loose casters should be fed into the swim at intervals to encourage the dace to feed on them. Bear in mind that if they are feeding deep it is likely that they are feeding on minute nymphs, which we cannot possibly imitate; and if so, we must attempt to wean them gradually away from feeding on this natural food to feeding on the chry-salids. This is not normally difficult as their natural greed, and the comparative ease with which the chrysalids can be taken, usually results in them changing their feeding habits sooner or later.

Sometimes more dace will be caught if the chrysalid is fished on the bottom, and for this it is only necessary to attach sufficient weight close to the hook to sink the chrysalid and hold it lightly on the bottom. One small weight should be sufficient in most swims. The float is then set at a slightly greater depth than the actual depth of the swim and held under the rod-tip on a tight line. If the weight has been correctly chosen the float will not move until a dace picks up the chrysalid. Then it will move quickly out of position, and the bite should be hit smartly.

In its later stages of development, just prior to the larva emerging as a fully-developed fly, the chrysalid is an even deadlier bait if the lower end of its thorax is carefully peeled away. This will reveal part of the body and the rear legs of the hatching fly, giving added attraction to the chrysalid because it now has an appearance of life. The methods of fishing it remain unchanged and it is equally effective whether fished on the surface or beneath it.

If chrysalids are not readily available, a small piece of floating crust can be an excellent substitute. This should be about fingernail size, and should be fished on a size 10 or 12 hook. A float is not essential, but if one is used a small 3–4in quill is ideal.

LIVE-FLY FISHING

Fishing for dace with a live fly—usually a bluebottle, greenfly, or housefly—is a method that is not often used, yet this bait can prove even more deadly than the chrysalid. A pint of maggots will provide enough flies for at least one fishing session if they are left in a warm place in a tin with a perforated lid until they begin to hatch out. For quicker results, a supply of casters should be obtained as these will turn into flies more quickly than the maggots. Once the flies have hatched out from the chrysalids they should be dampened lightly with water to prevent them flying away.

The method of fishing them is similar to that advised for fishing with the chrysalid. A small, sharp hook is essential, and should be inserted lightly through the upper part of the thorax. No weight should be used, and only a small quill float. Allow at least 2ft of line between float and hook. Dace will often feed madly on natural flies, and it is possible to take large catches of them with this bait.

If the dace fail to rise to the surface flies, it is worth trying the effect of fishing the fly beneath the surface. A dust-shot, lightly pinched on the line close to the hook, will normally provide sufficient weight to sink the fly, and the float can then be adjusted to fish the fly as a slow-sinking bait, or on the bottom. Both methods will lure dace and the angler should experiment, increasing the depth at which the fly is fished until the taking level is found.

METHODS FOR THE WINTER

When the colder weather denudes the shallows of their luxuriant weed-growth the dace tend to fall back into the deeper water of the slower-moving glides and pools, and are seldom seen close to the surface. During this period the bottom-fished maggot, chrysalid, or bread-bait will often prove the best method.

Again, both the slow-sinking style and the laying-on, or float-legering style, advised for roach can be used. Dace will some-times take a slow-sinking bait even on the coldest winter day, but there are other days when they seem to prefer the bait to be fished on the bottom. This is especially the case when the water is low and clear. In the depth of winter, when the temperature is near or below freezing-point, dace will be found most frequently in the deep pools, especially those that are fed by a brisk current. At this time of the year, good catches can often be made by laying-on with a piece of bread-paste roughly the size of a pea. During a spate, and for some time afterwards, worms and crust will often lure dace too, but whatever bait is used it is generally advisable to use a float. Dace are exceedingly difficult to catch on leger tackle as their bite is not usually prolonged enough to allow the average angler to strike it with any great chance of success.

TACTICS FOR THE SPECIMENS

Most of the larger dace I have taken from streams have been caught by totally different methods—methods which might seem more suited to chub fishing than to the quicksilver dace. The two largest, which weighed 10oz and 12oz, were caught with a whole lobworm fished on a 4lb line and a size 6 hook, and the only common denominator between the two captures was that the bait was larger than is normally used for dace, and that it was fished on the bottom.

Both factors would seem to indicate that the larger dace are more inclined to feed on larger items of food than small dace, and also more likely to pick their food up off the bottom. If so, it follows that, when hunting specimen fish, heavier bottom-fishing methods should be used rather than the lighter, slower-sinking styles generally used to catch dace. Small dace, like small chub and roach, tend to feed most frequently in the upper stratas of water, so that the bigger and heavier bait, which sinks quickly, is less vulnerable to attack by the smaller fish. In contrast, the maggot or chrysalid resembles closely the minute organisms upon which the smaller dace feed, and so are more likely to be taken by them. And while it is not possible to guarantee that only large dace will be caught if a big bait is used, certain it is that few if any of the small dace will be caught.

Some degree of selectivity should also be exercised in the choice of bait for the large dace. During and after a spate a worm is an excellent bait for them, but when the water is low a piece of flake, crust, paste, or cheese is to be preferred. The bread-baits are most effective during the winter and, generally speaking, flies seem to have only a limited appeal on other than the larger rivers. The two baits I would recommend above all others are the worm and paste.

Live-baits are not generally associated with dace fishing, and it would be an optimistic angler indeed who deliberately sought specimen dace with a live-bait. Nevertheless, there is some evidence to suggest that large dace are predatory, and I have actually seen one large dace caught with a live minnow.

I I

Angling for Rudd

THE NATURE OF THE FISH

THE RUDD is a gregarious fish that moves about in large shoals. It is not usually found in the small rivers and streams of England, but is quite common in Ireland, where it is often confused with the true roach which it closely resembles. It is found most abundantly in those streams which run into a lake containing large quantities of the species. Very rarely does one catch just one rudd, if you do you can be reasonably sure that there are others in the stream.

In appearance it is similar to the roach, but has several distinguishing features that make it easy to recognise. Its lower jaw juts out slightly beyond the upper one, and the dorsal fin is set further back than that of the roach. Its colouring is also more striking, more brilliant. Its back is usually jade green, its flanks silver, and its fins scarlet. To the practised eye it is easily distinguished from the roach.

The similarity between the two species extends to their feeding habits but, unlike roach, rudd often feed at surface level where they may be seen rising to sip in flies and other insects. During the summer they often shoal thickly in the fast water, but as the season advances they tend to fall back into the quieter, more placid swims. Slow-moving, reedy swims are favourite haunts of rudd, especially the larger specimens.

Like the roach, the smaller rudd can sometimes be caught speedily and in quantity, but the larger fish are not taken so easily. Nor are they as common, and any angler who catches a rudd of over 2lb can congratulate himself. Over 3lb they are outstanding fish, and very few anglers ever catch rudd of this weight—even from the larger waters. To catch a rudd of this size from a stream would indeed be a rare event.

The most effective baits are undoubtedly flies, both natural and artificial, the bread baits and, to a lesser extent, worms. The most commonly used bait is bread, but during the summer months, when insect life is most prolific, fly-fishing is probably the most rewarding method to use and, certainly one of the best methods of catching rudd rather than roach. Rudd rise much more freely than roach do.

FLY-FISHING

The first essential is to locate a feeding shoal by looking for signs of rising fish. The rudd may then be seen drifting to and fro just beneath the surface, and if they are rising from time to time daintily to sip in a struggling fly, the obvious course is to fish for them with a fly, rather than a sunken bait.

The light fly-fishing outfit previously recommended for roach and dace can be used for rudd, too. Both wet and dry flies will tempt them, but the dry fly is to be preferred when the rudd are actually rising, or can be seen close to the surface. The actual pattern of fly is not usually important as long as it is small and presented delicately. Greenwell's Glory, Pheasant Tail or Blue Dun should prove equally effective on most occasions but if the rudd are rising to an identifiable fly, such as an Iron Blue, one of the Olives, or even Mayflies, then the angler should definitely use an imitation. As with most forms of stream fishing, a stealthy approach and a deceptive presentation are the most important considerations. As long as the shoal is not scared it is often possible to catch large quantities of rudd with the artificial fly.

The methods of fishing the chrysalid or live fly on the surface, as described for dace fishing, are often equally deadly for rudd. Nor should live bluebottles, greenflies, or house-flies, fished on a small hook, be overlooked as they, too, are often accepted eagerly by feeding rudd.

When rudd cannot be seen rising it is more profitable to use a wet fly or nymph, and to fish it beneath the surface in one of the styles previously described. A small fly-spoon will also tempt them sometimes, but this method, and fly-fishing, are apt to lead to the capture of other species such as dace, chub and roach. However, an angler with knowledge of the water and who uses his powers of observation should be able to locate and identify rudd without too much difficulty.

FLOAT-FISHING METHODS

Inevitably there will be many days when no rudd can be seen rising, and when other methods of fishing can be more profitably used. Rudd are traditionally caught with a slow-sinking bait, but there are times when tradition must be put aside in favour of other methods better suited to fishing in small streams. There are also occasions, especially during the winter, when bottom-fishing will produce the best results, and the wise angler will always adapt his tactics to the needs of the moment.

The slow-sinking style, in which the deceptive action of the bait as it falls slowly down through the water is all-important, makes it necessary to use reasonably light tackle. Weight should be used sparingly, the line should be of the lowest breaking-strain which can safely be used, and the float both small and slim. My own outfit consists of a 12ft built-cane rod, a 2lb line, a 3–4in quill float and a size 12 hook.

The float is attached by both rings and set so that the bait will remain off bottom when it reaches maximum fall. The weight is then attached in such a way that the bait will sink slowly down through the water as the float travels downstream. This effect is achieved by placing the heaviest weight close to the float. Other, smaller weights are then attached as required, the smallest and lightest weight—generally a dust shot—being placed closest to the hook. If it is correctly weighted, the bait should sink slowly, and when it is fully sunken only the tip of the float will remain above the surface. Any unusual deviation in the action of the float, either while it is settling down in the water or when the bait is fully sunken, should be interpreted as a bite and the strike should be made smartly (see Fig 8).

This method is most effective in the deeper swims where the current is slowest, but it can also be used in the faster, shallower water provided the weights are adjusted to counter the increased pace of the current. This may entail moving one of the heavier weights closer to the hook and adjusting the depth at which the float is set in order to keep the bait up off the bottom in the shallower water; but if the rudd are shoaling in the shallow swims, as they often are during the early months of the season, it is obviously wise to concentrate on these swims.

This method of float-fishing can be used in all those swims in which the water is deep enough and where there is sufficient room to swim the float a reasonable distance downstream. When the swim is small, confined, and overgrown, it is often preferable to fish the bait steadily in one place. If so, the laying-on, or float-legering method, should be used. The bottom weight should be placed only an inch or so from the hook, and should be just heavy enough to hold the bait in position. The float is then set at a slightly greater depth than the water and fished either downstream or upstream, depending upon the nature of the swim. As always, the angler's first consideration must be to remain undetected, and if the swim can be fished more effectively by casting the tackle upstream then this method should be used in preference.

These bottom-fishing methods are, naturally, most productive when the rudd are feeding close to the bottom, which is increasingly the case as the season moves on into winter. They also frequently yield rudd of a better average size than those caught with the slow-sinking style, and one afternoon in late September, while fishing with bread-flake lightly legered on the bottom, I caught five rudd ranging from 1lb 5oz to 1lb 12oz, whereas on the previous day I had caught twenty-five smaller rudd from the same swim using a slow-sinking bait, coupled with periodic groundbaiting with dried bread-crumbs. For the larger rudd, no groundbait was used, apart from a few scraps of bread-flake. These two instances are further evidence that the methods that catch small fish do not usually catch many large ones, even though the two different sizes of fish often inhabit the same swim.

Soft white paste is also an excellent bait to use in conjunction with bottom-fishing as, being heavier than flake, it sinks more quickly and is therefore more likely to reach the bottom without being shredded to fragments by small rudd and minnows.

During periods of heavy rain, when the stream rises and the water rapidly becomes coloured, worms are a better bait for rudd than bread—though they are also attractive to perch and to chub —and anyone determined to fish for rudd while a spate is on should definitely try a small red-worm or brandling.

LEGERING

Rudd are extremely difficult to catch by legering unless the tackle is most carefully adjusted, as they are very shy biters and quickly drop a bait if they feel the slightest resistance. For this reason the rod chosen should at least have a flexible tip, and the leger weight should be only just heavy enough to sink the bait. A line of around 3lb breaking-strain should be strong enough in most circumstances.

Bites from the smaller fish are usually of short duration, and may be registered as no more than a slight twitch of the line. A keen eye, and quick reactions, are needed if the angler hopes to contact many of these bites. When flake is used, the strike should be made at the first indication of a bite but when a worm is used the rudd should be given a little more time. The bigger rudd take the bait more wholeheartedly; but on most occasions I prefer to use a float tackle for my rudd fishing.

TACTICS FOR THE SPECIMENS

Taking rod and bait in search of rudd is not a method that is often used in the larger rivers, but has obvious advantages in a small stream, where the opportunities of observing rudd and presenting a bait to them at close range are so much greater. It is not a method that is likely to catch a lot of rudd, but it can be an excellent way of singling out large specimens—provided the water is clear enough to permit accurate location of the fish.

The best time to use this method is when the water is low and clear and the weed-growth most abundant. Then, all along the course of the stream, there will be many swims which will hold big rudd, and in which they can sometimes be seen lying close to the cover afforded by a lily-pad or a bed of reed-mace. In these circumstances groundbait is unnecessary, and the angler's aim must be to cast a bait to the fish without disturbing it. Rudd are easily scared. A heavy footfall, or a shadow carelessly cast across the water, and the big, ghostly shapes of the rudd will fade slowly away into the depths, and there will be no second opportunity of catching one of them there that day.

The tackle I use for this style of fishing is my 12ft built-cane rod, a 4lb line, and a size 10 or 8 hook baited with a piece of bread-flake, or a small worm. The worm can be fished on a weightless cast, but flake should be weighted by one small weight, which should be just sufficient to overcome the natural buoyancy of the flake. The aim is to get it to sink slowly and naturally down through the water.

In some circumstances, as when the rudd are lying just under the surface, the bait can be fished without any weight so that it will float. Rudd will sometimes rise to suck in a bait fished in this manner, provided that it is carefully presented. In many swims it is wise policy to make use of the current to drift the flake down to the rudd; but if there is sufficient cover to permit a close approach it is sometimes possible to catch one by virtually lowering the bait on to its nose.

I used this tactic one summer afternoon to catch a rudd that was lying close to a bed of lilies in company with two others. They looked big—probably in excess of 2lb—and making use of the cover afforded by a thick bed of reed-mace that grew out over the swim, I squeezed a thumb-nail-sized piece of flake around a size 8 hook, thrust the rod carefully through the intervening reeds, and lowered the flake on to the water.

After a moment's hesitation, when it seemed that the flake would drift back downstream untouched, one of the rudd rose slowly to the surface and sucked the flake in. I struck quickly and held on as the big rudd strove to dive into lilies. The tackle proved equal to the task, and a few seconds later I netted a beautiful fish, weighing 2lb 4oz, one of the largest rudd I have ever caught from a stream.

Even when rudd cannot be seen, the same tactics can still be used, if the bait is tossed or lowered into the swim and the line watched for that tell-tale twitching that indicates a bite. A float can be used, if desired, but is often more of an encumbrance than a help in this style of fishing. Where a float is essential in order to drift the bait downstream, a twig or a feather should be used—or even a piece of crust. In very clear streams a float is apt to be conspicuous, and may cast an alarming shadow, whereas a twig, feather, or piece of crust are less likely to scare the rudd.

Another way of catching these bigger rudd is to choose a swim that is known to contain them and to fish a bait steadily on the bottom. A large piece of flake or paste is best, and groundbaiting should be confined to a few scraps of the hook-bait. Some small rudd may, even then, still be caught but so long as the angler refrains from saturating the swim with fine cloud-bait, the bulk of the rudd he catches will be larger than average, and may even include some of specimen size. Sometimes these large rudd are caught quickly but, more often, there will be days when the angler must be prepared to wait, as patiently as he can and perhaps for several hours, for the rudd to start feeding.

12

Angling for Bream

THE NATURE OF THE FISH

THE BREAM is a slow-moving, ponderous fish that seeks its food mainly on the bottom. It is seldom found in very fast water, except during the very early months of the season, but prefers the slower-moving deeper parts of the stream where the current is sluggish and where it can find the larvae, nymphs, and vegetable matter upon which it feeds. It is not equipped for speed or for hunting down other fish and is rarely caught with a live-bait, fly or spinner.

Like the roach and the rudd, it has silvery flanks, but there the resemblance ends. It is thinner across the back, but deep-bodied and very slimy. Its fins are a dull, neutral colour; its eyes a pale yellow. It is also a much larger fish than either the roach or rudd. A bream weighing 2lb is only a modest specimen and in some small rivers and streams these fish may be caught up to 4lb, or even 5 or 6lb. Bream of this size are usually only found in any quantity in streams that run into a larger river or lake that contains specimen bream, and very rarely in fast, rocky streams.

The baits which will catch bream can be narrowed down to worms, bread, maggots, and to a lesser degree, the seed-baits. Of these, maggots are possibly the most deadly, provided that they are used in quantity and it is possible to avoid the minnows. Brandlings or red-worms are more killing when the water is coloured. In most streams both bread and the seed-baits must be persisted with before any worthwhile results can be expected. In contrast, maggots and worms will lure bream almost anywhere— even in waters where they have not been used before.

Normally, it is not too difficult to locate bream, even though they are seldom seen lying close to the surface. In streams which have a great variety of different swims the deeper pools are the most likely places. In those with a more sedate, even flow, the bream will be more widespread, but will seldom be far away from a reasonable depth of water.

When the water is low and clear they can sometimes be seen moving slowly from swim to swim in small compact shoals, sometimes in odd groups of up to half-a-dozen fish, and sometimes in larger shoals of up to thirty or more. Individual specimens can also be spotted and tracked down in this way.

In streams which are not clear enough, or are too deep to permit observations to be made, the angler should try to locate the species by exploring with rod and bait. If this is done patiently and conscientiously a picture will gradually be built up which will enable him to locate the bream with surprising accuracy. Groundbait, introduced in quantity into selected swims, will also help to narrow down the area of search tremendously.

LOW-WATER TACTICS

Let us begin the search for bream in the month of June when the temperature is high and bream may still be seen around the fringes of the fast water—unmistakably large, flat-sided shapes that seem scarcely to move. If so, this is not the time for traditional bream-fishing methods of groundbaiting and fishing the bait on the bottom, but an opportunity to make a quick capture of which full use should be made.

The Mark VI Avon rod, a 4lb line and a size 8 hook baited with a worm, is the tackle we shall use, and to avoid scaring the bream we stay downstream and flick the worm so that it lands close but upstream of them, taking care that the line does not fall across their backs. Bream are not quick-moving fish like trout, but if they see the worm falling slowly down through the current close to them there is an excellent chance that one of them will take it.

On one occasion I spotted a small shoal of bream patrolling

slowly upstream through a shallow swim dotted with clumps of lilies, and tossed a few brandlings upstream to them. At once they became alerted to the worms, and as they drifted down through the clear water the bream moved slowly across the current to intercept them. I then baited my hook with a brandling and flicked it upstream to the shoal. One of the bream took it immediately, and was promptly hooked, brought back downstream and netted. A few minutes later another was landed by the same method, shortly after which the shoal moved off rapidly, no doubt alarmed by the sudden disappearance of two of its members. The two captured bream weighed 4lb 8oz and 4lb 10oz—very good bream for that little stream.

There are times, too, when bream lying close to the surface can be caught by drifting a bait downstream to them—provided the swim is long enough and there is some cover on the banks behind which the angler can hide. This method of spotting the bream and presenting a bait to them may be unusual, but it can enable one to catch them under conditions of low, clear water and bright sunshine which keep many anglers away from the waterside. Even the sunshine can then be advantageous, as it enables the angler to see the bream more easily, and to watch their every movement. And on subsequent occasions, when the light is poor, the angler will know where bream are most likely to be and can fish carefully up the stream, casting his bait into every spot where he has previously seen them.

Sometimes, of course, no bream can be seen, or the water is too highly coloured to permit accurate observation. Or one may even work carefully over all the well-known swims and still not catch a single bream. This may be because they are not feeding at the time, in which case they may sometimes be encouraged to do so by dropping in a little groundbait at carefully chosen places. A heavy mixture of wheatmeal and maggots, or brandlings, is ideal. A ball of this mixture is tossed into the chosen swim and left for the bream to find. If, when the angler returns to this swim, he finds the bream feeding confidently on the groundbait there will be an excellent chance of catching one of them.

*A stretch of the
Whitewater river
near Kilkeel,
Co Down—a
typical mountain
stream that rises
and falls rapidly
and has excellent
runs of sea-trout
and salmon*

Page 118 (above) *A 4½lb bream taken on brandling from a small stream;* (below) *a specimen roach of 2lb 2oz which took a bread-crust bait in a Midlands brook*

FLOAT-FISHING METHODS FOR DEEP WATER

In the course of time the best bream swims become well-known, and when the water has sufficient depth the more normal methods of fishing for bream with float tackle should be employed. A slow-sinking style is not often used, unless the bream are feeding off-bottom, because this is more likely to attract small roach and rudd, and the method most likely to tempt the wary bream is a bait fished on the bottom, or just tripping along it.

Here, again, the angler can often influence the bream's feeding pattern by varying the pattern and quantity of his groundbaiting. If a loose mixture which will quickly disintegrate is used, it is likely that the bream will begin to feed off the bottom, in company with any other fish there may be in the swim. So, if the angler wishes to catch bream only, it is usually better to use a heavier groundbait which will sink quickly and thus encourage the bream to continue feeding on the bottom, where they are most accustomed to picking up their food.

The next step is to rig the tackle in such a way that it will carry the bait quickly down to the bottom, and there are several ways of doing this. One is to attach sufficient weight, about a foot from the hook, to sink the bait, and to adjust the float so that it will lie flat when the bait is fully sunken. The tackle is then cast into the swim and the float held on a tight line underneath the rod-tip. When a bream takes the bait the float will sail smoothly away, and few bream should be missed (Fig 13).

Float-legering, which makes use of a sliding-link, is an alternative method of fishing the bait on the bottom, and the one that many anglers prefer. It is wise, however, to avoid using an excessive amount of weight, as this might be detected by the bream and lead to shy bites which will be difficult to hit successfully.

Line strength should be related to the prevailing conditions, and while in some swims a 3lb breaking-strain line will be strong enough, in others it may be wiser to use a much stronger line. When the bait is fished lying on the bottom the stronger line can

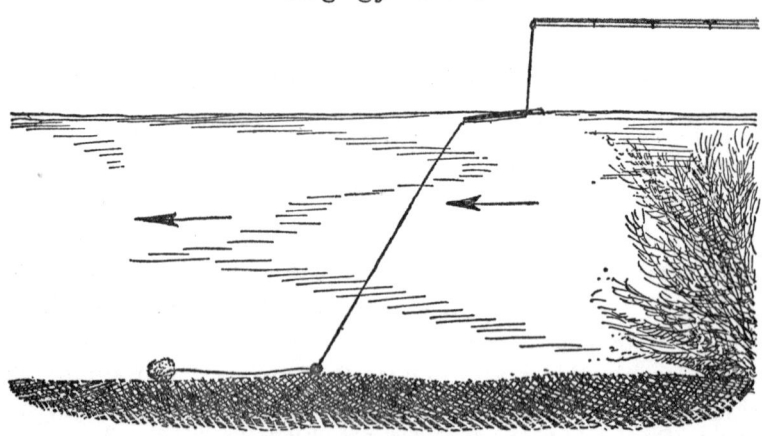

Fig 13 *Bottom-fishing tackle for bream, in the traditional and still very effective style. Alternatively, the float leger style (Fig 3), or the laying-on style (Fig 9) can be used*

be used without fear of it being detected by the bream, and bites can be struck with a much greater degree of confidence. Bream are not great fighters, but it is always risky to use a fine line in a snaggy overgrown swim.

LEGERING

Legering can be used to catch bream in almost any swim, and is particularly suitable where conditions make it difficult to use a float, and during the after-spate period when the water is high and coloured.

This style of fishing is best undertaken with a Mark IV Avon rod, or other rod of similar design, a 4lb breaking-strain line, and a link leger. Provided the weight is correctly chosen to just sink the bait, most bream bites on the leger are quite easy to hit. The line tightens slowly to the rod-tip, giving an unmistakable signal which should seldom be missed.

TACTICS FOR THE SPECIMENS

Most of the large bream caught in recent years have been taken from still-waters, and it is doubtful whether there are many small rivers or streams holding really large bream. In most streams a bream weighing 5lb would be an outstanding specimen, so the angler seeking bream in these waters should not set his sights too high. Occasionally, bream weighing 6, or even 7lb, might be caught from the best waters, but the average specimen will certainly weigh much less.

One method by which these larger fish can be caught—by spotting them and tossing a bait to them on a floatless line—has already been described and is one of the most effective methods of catching specimen fish from streams. It is not always possible to use it, however, and another often productive method is to explore each likely swim with a bait fished on a light leger tackle in the hope that any large bream lying in the swim will be tempted. No groundbait is needed, and a recommended bait is a large lobworm. Inevitably, other fish will be caught, but occasionally a large bream will pick up a bait fished in this way. I have caught several like this, including one weighing 6lb 2oz from a small tributary of the Blackwater river that runs into Lough Neagh, in County Armagh, Ulster.

Remaining quietly in one swim, and using groundbait, will also produce large bream; and the longer one spends fishing the selected swim the more likely it is that the larger bream will eventually move in to feed. Bream tend to move about in shoals composed of fish of about the same size, so that if small bream, in the $\frac{1}{2}$–1lb category, are caught it is extremely unlikely that any really large bream will be caught at the same time. Once these smaller fish have moved out, however, the larger fish will often move in, and although the bites will become less frequent the bream caught will usually be much bigger.

So do not get impatient if bites become infrequent, as this may mean that the smaller bream have become sated with food and moved out of the swim. The water will then be less disturbed and this is the time for the angler to remain quiet and concealed, bait up with a large lobworm and be prepared to wait for that one bite that could mean a specimen bream.

The best times are undoubtedly at dawn, or at dusk; and preferably when there is some colour in the water. And if the stream runs into a lake or a large river, it will pay to concentrate on the mouth of the stream where the water is deep and sluggish. More large bream are likely to be found here than in the upper reaches of the stream.

13

Angling for Pike

THE NATURE OF THE FISH

THE PIKE could truly be called the leviathan of the stream. It is by far the largest of all the fish that inhabit these small waters and is a true predator, the greater part of its diet consisting of other fish. Even the young of its own species are not immune.

The majority of pike caught range from small jacks to fish of around 10lb, but individual specimens weighing over 20lb are occasionally landed. Much depends upon the amount of food available and the nature of the water. Some streams do not contain pike at all, while in others they are quite common.

Its size and appearance make the pike easy to recognise. A long, lean fish, with an aggressive-looking bony head, its colouring is dappled green and yellow—a combination that merges well with the weeds in which it often lies in ambush, awaiting the passing of any unwary roach, rudd, dace or perch. It is capable of a quick burst of speed and its forward-looking eyes enable it to hunt by sight—although, like all fish, it can also detect its prey by scent. Pike are greatly attracted by movement—a fact which the angler can turn to his benefit when seeking them.

The sheer size of the pike suggests that it should be easy to locate within the narrow waters of a stream, but this is not always so. True, when it is actively hunting down its prey it can easily be found, either by the signs of alarm exhibited by the hunted fish, or by the disturbance it creates as it moves through the water; but when it is not hunting it can be as difficult to locate as other species sometimes are. In the summer, when the streams are thickly overgrown with dense beds of weed, the pike often lies unseen beneath them, almost unapproachable in its weedy lair. It also lies under debris, the overhanging branches of trees, and under tree roots. It is rarely found in fast, shallow water—unless it is hunting minnows—and favours the deeper water of the pools where it is able to conceal itself. So well is it camouflaged that when motionless it is extremely difficult to see, and it is remarkable how such a large fish can often remain undetected in a small stream. Yet it can, and does.

The pike is not a shoal fish. Like most predators, it hunts alone, and may even have its own little domain from which it will drive out any intruder. Contrary to popular opinion, it is not as destructive of fish life as it is often reputed to be, for pike have periods when they eat little or nothing, and other fish are well aware of this. I have often seen pike lying quietly in a swim, with other fish upon which it normally preys, in close attendance; and yet the pike has not exhibited the slightest sign of interest. In some way the other fish sense that the pike is not in a feeding mood, and hunter and hunted then share the same little domain in apparent harmony. Yet when the pike is actively hunting it quickly generates alarm, and other fish rapidly make off to a safe hiding place.

These different moods must obviously affect the angler's chances of success. When the pike is lying dormant and not feeding, it can be more difficult to entice than any other fish; but when it is actively seeking food it can often be caught quite easily, and can even become a nuisance to the seeker of other, smaller fish. There will be occasions when a pike will remain completely indifferent to the most carefully presented bait or spinner—and others when it will pursue them with almost suicidal zest, rudely dispersing all other fish in the vicinity.

PIKE CALL FOR STRONG TACKLE

Each fish has its season, and for me there is no better time to seek the pike than during the dark winter months. The Mark IV Avon and the roach rod are put aside, and their place taken by rods and tackle more suited to the strenuous task of catching pike.

The snaggy, overgrown nature of many streams leaves little scope for finesse. The tackle must be strong throughout, and a well-balanced outfit will consist of a 10ft pike rod, and a line of between 10 and 12lb breaking-strain. I sometimes use a Mark IV carp rod and an 8lb line, but the stronger outfit is preferable from the point of view of striking and setting the hooks, and for holding the pike out of the snags. The angler must make his own choice, based upon the nature of the stream and the problem of landing the pike. It is bad angling to risk fishing with a weak line because this can result in the pike breaking free with a treble hook or spinner embedded in its mouth.

SPINNING

There are several ways of catching pike from a stream, and one of the most productive and enjoyable methods is to spin for them. This is an all-action method of fishing that calls for some accurate casting, but it will often catch a lot of pike and will certainly reveal where others are lying.

Many different kinds of spinners are available—my own favourite is a 1½in wobbling spoon—and they can be obtained in various colours though I do not think that colour is of any real significance. It is the action imparted to the spinner that lures the pike. The larger spoon does, however, reduce considerably the number of perch caught.

When spinning for pike, it is a good plan to start at the downstream end of the water and work slowly upstream. During the late autumn most, if not all, of the weeds have vanished and it is inadvisable to spin downstream as the forward-looking eyes of the pike will quickly detect anyone standing on the bank above it. The angler who remains downstream of the pike, casting his spinner upstream in front of him, is far more likely to be successful.

Long casting is rarely possible, or necessary. The rapid changes in direction taken by most streams, and the variety of alternating deeps and shallows, means that most casts have to be short but accurate. The angler must learn how to cast the spoon up in between, and under, over-hanging branches of trees; how to avoid underwater snags in the form of sunken branches; and when to retrieve the spoon at a fast or a slow pace. Tackle losses must be regarded as an occupational risk, but can certainly be cut down if the angler has learned through observation where the worst of the snags are, and is skilful enough to be able to cast the spoon into a confined place. It is, of course, easier to bypass these difficult swims, but many pike will then be missed.

More pike are likely to be found lying in ambush than in open water, and if the spoon is wound back close to the bank, or close to any weed-beds or snags there may be in the swim, it is more likely to find a taker. Later on, experience will indicate which swims are most likely to contain pike, and which seldom hold them.

WOBBLING THE SPRAT

Another method of tempting pike is the wobbled sprat. This is mounted on a wire trace which is threaded in at the vent and drawn out of the mouth. A treble hook is then attached to the trace at the vent, and a swivel at the other end. The trace is then secured to the reel line, with an anti-kink lead on the line just above the swivel. A single hook inserted into the mouth of the sprat will prevent it from getting torn by the trace, and will also add hooking power to the tackle (Fig 14).

The method of working the sprat is to cast it upstream and work it back slowly in an erratic manner imitative of an injured fish. The sprat can also be made to dive and wobble—movements

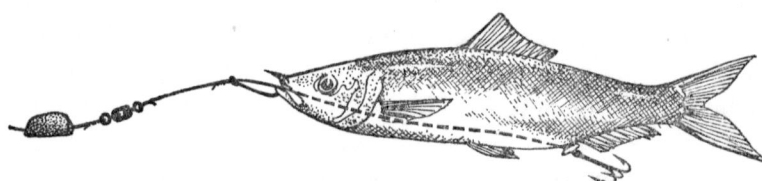

Fig 14   *Tackle for fishing with a sprat, or other dead-bait—a most effective method for pike*

126

to which pike often react by striking fiercely at the sprat. The lifelike appearance and action of the sprat make it more attractive to the pike than a metal spoon, and a small dead rudd or roach can be used when sprats are not available.

LIVE-BAITING

Basically, there are two methods of live-baiting which can be applied to streams. One is to take rod and bait in search of feeding pike; the other is to remain in one place and steadily fish the live-bait in the hope that a pike will be attracted to it.

The first method should not be despised. When pike are on the rampage it can be a deadly method—especially if the pike can be seen. There is no guarantee that the pike will take the bait, but at least the angler knows that his bait is being fished where it is most likely to be taken.

Several different baits can be used, the most obvious being the minnow, though a gudgeon, small roach, rudd, or dace can be equally effective. My method is to lip-hook the bait, using an eyed hook, size 4 at least. A float, which should just support the bait, can also be used, though I usually prefer to fish without one.

When the pike has been spotted the bait is cast upstream to land as close as possible to the fish, and preferably just upstream of it. Quite often the splash caused by the bait hitting the water is sufficient to alert the pike and it will often grab the bait instantly. If it does not the cast should be repeated several times from slightly different angles. Sometimes a pike will appear completely indifferent to a bait, but will grab it quickly when it is presented in a slightly different way. If these tactics fail, the pike should be left alone and revisited later. There are many occasions when a bait will be refused early in the day and taken quickly later on.

If a live-bait is not readily obtainable, a large worm can be used. Pike in small streams seem partial to a worm, especially if it is given an attractive spinning or wobbling movement. If the worm is cast upstream and then rapidly retrieved, it will wobble and undulate in a most attractive manner, and a pike will often snap it up as it passes by. Occasionally, too, a pike will pick up a worm from the bottom; but bottom-fishing with a worm is not a method to be recommended for catching pike.

The more static methods of live-baiting call for a totally different approach and technique. The angler usually has a prior knowledge of where he can expect to find a pike, and fishes his live-bait steadily in that one place in the hope that the pike will eventually be tempted to seize it. There are several ways of doing this. One is to use a simple link-leger tackle, to which is attached either a large single hook or a set of treble hooks. The weight is attached to the link as previously described, but should be just sufficient to hold the bait in place, and no more (Fig 15).

The live-bait is then attached to the hook and the tackle carefully lowered into the swim close to where the pike is lying. Sometimes it is seized immediately. More often a waiting period must be endured before the pike takes the bait. Sometimes, of course, the pike refuses to be tempted, and after a reasonable wait it may be better to move on and try another place.

Another method is to fish the live-bait on a float tackle using a float which is capable of supporting the bait. A small quill float will be big enough to support a minnow, but a much larger one

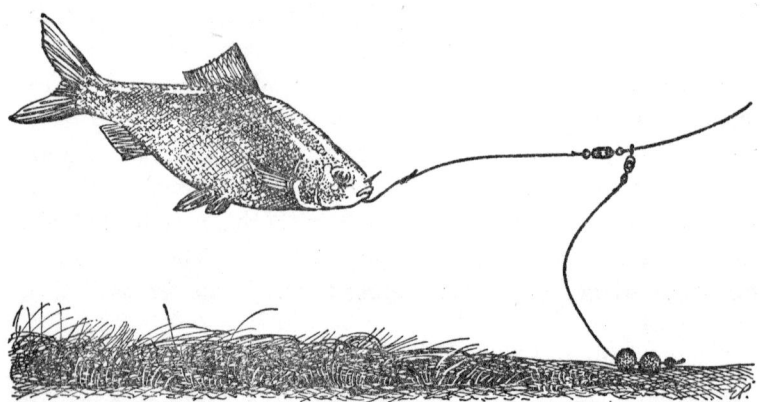

Fig 15   *A simple leger set-up for fishing a small live-bait. A running link is used with a swivel instead of a stop. The live-bait is lip-hooked with either a large single or treble hook*

will be needed if a large roach or rudd live-bait is used. A slim, cork-bodied float is excellent for use with the smaller live-baits. Pike are not as sensitive to tackle resistance as some other species, but when they are not particularly hungry they can be put off by a large float or an excessive amount of weight. It is only necessary to use enough weight to sink the bait to the required depth, which should be roughly around mid-water level. The pike is more likely to see it then than if it were fished on the bottom.

The live-bait itself can be attached to the hook in several ways. The simplest and most humane way is to lip-hook it, though this does involve some loss of hooking power. The most common method is to use two sets of hooks, one of which is attached to the bait close to its gills, and the other close to the roots of its dorsal fin. This method results in a higher proportion of hooked pike but can also be the cause of deep hooking. Bearing in mind that the pike seizes its prey across the body and then swallows it head first, it seems best to position the hooks so that an instantaneous strike can be made. This is best achieved by placing one set of trebles close to the dorsal fin and the other close to the tail. Alternatively, single hooks can be used in place of the trebles. Again, there is some loss of hooking power, but the single hooks are less likely to damage the bait and can also be extracted more easily than the trebles (Fig 16).

There is no doubt that these methods of using a live-bait attract the larger pike, which are not often interested in the smaller items of food. Roach or rudd up to a pound in weight

Fig 16 *An effective live-baiting rig which makes use of two large single hooks instead of the trebles generally used. The positioning of the hooks permits an instantaneous strike*

or more can be used, as these are easily consumed by a large pike, and even the smaller ones will occasionally take them.

Those anglers who find live-baiting repugnant should use a dead-bait. This is fished on two sets of treble hooks, one of which is placed close to the dorsal fin and the other close to the tail. No float is necessary. The bait is simply cast or lowered into the swim and left there for the pike to find.

This method requires more patience than I can usually muster, and I prefer the more active method of seeking pike with a spinner or live-bait. They are more likely, in my experience, to succumb to a moving bait than to a static one, and it is more exciting to take rod and bait and go in search of them.

TACTICS FOR THE SPECIMENS

Really big pike, in the 20–30lb category, are not often caught from the smaller rivers and streams and any pike over 5–10lb should be regarded as a big fish. Pike over 20lb are true specimens anywhere, and only the best of streams will produce them.

The methods outlined will all catch these larger pike and it is difficult to pin-point any one as being superior to another. In general, though, the larger the pike the more likely it is to succumb to a larger bait, and the angler who has set his mind on catching a specimen should use larger spinners, or larger baits than he would normally employ. Large pike will take small spinners and small baits, but the chances are that most of those caught with the smaller lures and baits will be small to medium-sized fish.

As with all forms of specimen hunting, the most important step is to locate the large pike. They will seldom be far away from cover, and in the summer they often lie concealed beneath thick weed-beds. In winter, they are more likely to be found in the deeper pools—especially if the pool is overhung by a tree.

Obviously, the most favourable time to seek them is when they are actively hunting down their prey. Otherwise, the angler will need to spend some time exploring all likely places, either with a spinner or with a bait fished on a leger or paternoster tackle. Of all the recognised methods, live-baiting is possibly the most effective for large pike, with wobbling a large dead-bait a close second. The retrieve in both cases should always be made slowly as a big pike is seldom inclined to chase a bait.

Large pike are best sought from late autumn onwards, the spring months being possibly the best time of all. Even then, there will be days when pike are simply not interested in food, but if the angler persists sooner or later the pike will feed, and when it does its greed makes it one of the easiest fish to hook— if not to land.

14

Angling for Sea-Trout

THE NATURE OF THE FISH

THE SEA-TROUT is spawned during the winter in shallow water. After about two years' growth in the river, it moves downstream to the sea and at this stage of its life it is more silvery than the brown trout and liberally dotted with black spots. In the richer pastures of the sea it grows rapidly, and by the time it returns to its parent river it is ready to spawn. Each year afterwards, for as long as it lives, it will obey this urge to move back into the river; and each year it will have grown bigger and stronger. In many rivers sea-trout make their first ascent when they are roughly the size of a herring. Fish of this size are often numerous, but sea-trout making their second or third run up the rivers are much larger. Fish weighing 2lb are quite common in many sea-trout rivers, and much larger specimens, up to 10lb or more, are caught from some rivers.

The adult sea-trout, which should not be confused with the duller brown trout, is a beautiful fish with flanks of beaten silver, sometimes suffused with pink or mauve, and liberally dotted with black spots. Its appearance makes this clean, streamlined, quicksilver fish of the deep ocean currents seem almost alien in fresh water. During the day it often lies invisible beneath the steely ripples of the fast water, or in the deepest recesses of some swirling pool. Like all trout, it has the ability to efface itself completely, and it is possible to peer down into the clear water and yet not be able to discern it. But if a fly, spinner, or worm is cast into the swim, the sea-trout will often strike. There is a tug on the line, a glimpse of a silvery flank turning in the current, and the fight is on.

It is often said that no fish fights as hard as the sea-trout, and certainly a sea-trout fresh in from the sea has few equals in this respect. Even the smallest of sea-trout often surprises the beginner with its electrifying runs and leaps, while a bigger fish will fight to the last, often leaping from the water shaking its head, and describing a shimmering arc in the air before falling back into the water to renew its energetic rushes and dives. Even in large rivers the sea-trout is always an adversary to respect, and in small, overgrown rivers and streams it provides the sternest challenge the angler is likely to meet—apart, perhaps, from that offered by the salmon.

METHODS FOR DAYLIGHT HOURS

Traditionally, most serious sea-trout fishing is done at night, and when the water is low and clear there is no doubt that late evening and on into the night is the best time to seek them. At this time, pools and glides that seemed devoid of fish beneath the bright, penetrating rays of the sun suddenly become alive with the tell-tale movements of unseen sea-trout. Nevertheless, sea-trout can be caught in the daytime—especially from the smaller, overgrown waters—provided the angler fishes quietly upstream.

A variety of methods, including fly-fishing, spinning, and up-stream worming can be used, but conditions may restrict the choice to either spinning or worming, both of which can be equally effective.

Spinning

Spinning for sea-trout is usually confined to periods when the water is relatively high and coloured, but this is by no means essential and the method is well worth a trial even when the water is low. The tackle and techniques recommended for spinning for brown trout can be used, as long as the tackle is related to the prevailing conditions and the probable size of the sea-trout. In streams in which the average size of the sea-trout is between ½lb and 2lb, a light outfit consisting of an 8½ft rod, a 4lb line, and a

1in spinner should be strong enough in most circumstances; but if the stream is known to contain really big sea-trout from 2lb upwards a much stronger outfit will be needed.

Tactics are important. Downstream spinning is rarely possible or advisable, and it is a good practice to start at the downstream end of the fishery and work up. Sometimes it is possible to start at the estuary itself, and during the early weeks of the sea-trout run in July this is often the best place to begin. As the season wears on, more and more sea-trout will penetrate further up the river and into its tributaries, and it is then that the most productive period of sea-trout fishing may be enjoyed. Each pool, glide and stickle; each twist and bend in the river may hold its quota of sea-trout, and the angler who works slowly and patiently upstream, casting his spinner into every likely spot, should catch some of them. On a good day he might catch many.

When spinning up fast-flowing rocky streams, a high-speed retrieve is essential to get the spinner working properly through the fast water and keep it clear of the rocks. The fast retrieve will not deter the sea-trout from striking. It has a keen eye and swift reactions, and the spinner is slow by comparison.

Wet-Fly Fishing

On some small rivers and streams opportunities for orthodox fly-fishing are severely restricted by the overgrowth, but wherever clearer stretches of water occur it is pleasant to use the fly in preference to the spinner or worm.

Again, tackle should be strong enough to handle the largest fish likely to be caught, but during the brightest hours of the day some concession has to be made if the fly is to be effectively presented. So, unless the stream is known to hold some really large sea-trout, the cast should be tapered down to about 3lb breaking-strain, and the flies should be smaller than those one would use at night: flies tied on size 10 or size 12 hooks will be most suitable. These will usually be wet flies as sea-trout do not normally rise as freely to the dry fly as the brown trout. There are of course, exceptions to this general rule, but the majority of sea-trout are caught on the wet fly.

Page 135 (above) *Fishing up an overgrown stream in mid-summer. Note how the angler makes use of natural cover and keeps well back from the edge of the stream; (below) winter fishing for chub under a mat of debris. Again keeping well back from the bank, the angler holds the line in his left hand to detect bites by feel as well as by sight*

Page 136 *A 3lb
brown trout taken
from a small
stream on a gold
Mepps spinner*

Local patterns of wet flies should, of course, be given preference, but old favourites like Mallard and Claret, Silver Butcher, Peter Ross and Teal and Silver are always worth trying. Sea-trout feed extensively on other smaller fish, and almost any fly with a glint of silver or gold on its body is likely to attract them when they are in a feeding mood.

Some anglers use two wet flies on a cast, but I prefer only one, and to fish it upstream on a short line. Long casts are seldom necessary in the smaller rivers and streams. The depth at which the fly is fished is often said to be critical, and to be governed by temperature, and even by the time of day. My advice is to relate the depth at which the fly is fished to the nature of the swim, and, where possible, to the observed feeding pattern of the fish. When fishing fast, shallow water which, at its deepest point, is probably only a foot or so deep, there is obviously no need to fish the fly deep since it will be easily seen by the sea-trout. This is also true when the sea-trout can be seen close to the surface in the deeper water.

When sea-trout are lying closer to the bottom the fly should obviously be fished deeper—at least to around mid-water level. A little fine wire wound around the body of the fly will quicken the rate of descent when fishing the faster, deeper swims.

Opportunities for downstream wet-fly fishing will be limited to those areas where there is sufficient depth and breadth of water to allow the method to be used without scaring the fish, and in the majority of streams the upstream method will generally be found the most effective.

NIGHT FISHING

While day-time fishing can often be rewarding, there is no doubt that the best time to catch sea-trout is when the light is fading from the sky—especially when the water is low and clear; but night fishing is best done in rivers and streams where the banks are reasonably clean. Trees, bushes, and reeds can create serious casting problems at night, and the wise angler will visit the area in which he intends to fish well before dusk, noting the

I

obstacles to be avoided and choosing a position from which he will be able to cast without fear of getting his tackle snarled up. He will also ascertain, by experiment, the maximum length of line he needs to cast to reach the water close to the opposite bank, and so avoid overcasting and getting caught up on overhanging vegetation. The depth of the chosen swim should also be plumbed and the cast made up accordingly.

In general, more sea-trout can be caught from shallow swims during the hours of darkness than in daylight. As sea-trout occupying these swims usually betray their presence, there is no need to fish the fly deep and a greased cast that will allow it to be fished just beneath the surface will be the best tactics. Otherwise, the fly should be fished deeper and slower, and a bigger fly used. A fly tied on a size 8 or size 6 hook is none too big, as most of the really big sea-trout are caught at night.

Night fishing is vastly different from any other kind of fishing. It demands intense concentration and almost everything has to be done by feel and instinct. The angler who knows his water well will be able to visualise the swims in his mind's eye—even to the extent of knowing how and where his fly is working—so that when the 'take' comes he is ready to strike. The angler whose mind is not attuned in this way will fish blindly, not knowing where his fly is or how it is behaving. His fishing will lack confidence, and he is unlikely to meet with much success.

It is helpful to hold the rod up against the evening sky so that the tip, and the downward sweep of the line can be observed and checked at every stage of its progress as the fly swings round and down. A finger held lightly on the line will also help to detect that tell-tale tremor, the slight pull, that could indicate a 'take'. Absolute concentration is vital, as is an instinctive ability to sense the slightest movement of the line.

When the trout is hooked, knowledge of the swim is invaluable, because the direction of the pull at the rod-tip alone will reveal which way the trout is heading. The net, too, must be ready for instant use the moment the struggling fish is drawn into the side.

At the end of each cast the line should be withdrawn carefully with the left hand until most of it is taken in. The rest can then be lifted off the water and re-cast in one simple movement. It is risky, and usually unnecessary, to indulge in false casting in these circumstances, as this will only increase the risk of getting the fly hung up on a bush or—even worse—around the angler's neck.

It is a strange, even eerie experience, to fish for sea-trout at night, but once the angler has sampled its fascination he is likely to return again and again to that river in which he had his first encounter with these game fighters from the sea.

15

Angling for Salmon

THE NATURE OF THE FISH

THE SALMON starts its life just as the sea-trout does—as a tiny
fish which hatches from eggs deposited on the gravelly shallows
by the hen fish returning to its parent river after a long sojourn
in the sea. At this stage the newly-hatched fry is known as an
alevin; and later, when it has attained a length of a few inches, as
a parr. After two years or so in the river, during which time it
can be caught easily with fly, spinner or worm, the parr becomes
silvery in colour and is then known as a smolt. Like the sea-trout,
it now begins to feel the call of the sea, and finally heads out into
the deep ocean where it remains until the following year, or
perhaps the year after. Those that return to their parent river
after only a year in the sea are known as grilse, and usually weigh
between 5 and 7lb. Grilse which survive this first run back up
the river return once more to the sea, to return again the following
year along with other salmon which have spent two or more
winters in the sea. They now weigh 10lb or more and are truly
salmon.

Like sea-trout, adult salmon are found only in those streams
that run into the sea, and only in these when they are running up
to spawn. Opportunities of catching salmon are therefore limited
to those periods—which may be in spring, mid-summer or late
autumn, depending upon the location of the stream and the height
of the water. If the stream is low, the salmon will remain in the
estuary, coming in with the tide but never venturing far upstream
until the rains bring the river up in spate. Then, under cover of

the thick, brown water, they begin their trek upstream to the spawning beds, where they will repeat the yearly ritual of spawning. Those that survive the journey often subsequently die of exhaustion. A few, more fortunate, fall back downstream again and are carried out to sea, there to spend another year of their lives before returning to the river, bigger and stronger than ever.

FINDING A RIVER

The best of salmon rivers are jealously preserved and the casual visitor will usually find it difficult to get permission to fish. But there are also many small, insignificant-looking rivers and streams around the coasts of the British Isles from which salmon can sometimes be caught, some of the finest being located along the coasts of Ireland and Scotland.

Some of these streams are little more than burns scarcely over a foot wide in places. Yet salmon can, and do, penetrate upstream into them, and their very smallness is often their best guarantee of protection. The average angler pays them little heed, thinking they are too small to contain salmon, but the few who know better and are prepared to put up with discomfort can sometimes reap a rich reward in the shape of a fat, gleaming salmon. And there is no finer thrill than to hook a salmon; no finer fish than a full-grown salmon fresh in from the sea.

The ideal time to seek salmon is when a stream is running high after a spate, and before poachers and other enemies of salmon have decimated the stock. Small streams rise and fall quickly, and in many cases the water will be back to normal level within twenty-four hours. It is therefore vital to take advantage of the spate. The salmon, fresh in from the sea, is then more active and more easily caught, and likely to be found in many different swims. Later, when the water falls, it will survive only where there is sufficient water to cover it—in the deeper pools beneath over-hanging trees and bridge tunnels. Those that are trapped in shallow water will not long survive, and a long, dry spell will make salmon sluggish and almost impossible to catch.

The estuary and the deep pools in the lower reaches of the

river provide the most accessible fishing, but are almost always overcrowded and overfished, especially at holiday times. If you enjoy this kind of community fishing then join the happy throng; if not, discard all unnecessary equipment—including that new, two-handed salmon rod—equip yourself instead with a 9ft spinning rod, a fixed-spool reel loaded with 8lb line, a few large hooks (size 4 at least), baits and lures, or, alternatively, a fly-fishing outfit, and prepare yourself for a hard but exhilarating slog up into the upper regions of the stream. The chances are that you will encounter few other anglers, which means that the salmon, though fewer than in the lower reaches, will be largely undisturbed and therefore less difficult to catch.

METHODS TO USE

Now we are right back where we started, for the methods of fishing upstream recommended for trout and chub, are just as effective for taking salmon from small streams. Everything that has gone before—all the long hours of fishing and observing—have prepared you for this final moment of truth when you will attempt to catch the king of all fish. No matter if it does not match in size and power the larger fish of the big rivers. Within the confined waters of a stream a 7lb salmon will feel monstrous, and will provide a stern test of your skill with rod and line.

Fly-Fishing

But, first, a method must be chosen. Fly-fishing is possible in some streams, and perhaps the method to be preferred whenever practicable—although in many streams there is not room enough, nor sufficient breadth of water, to cast a fly in the manner employed on the larger rivers. This means that a lighter outfit and a shorter fly-fishing rod will usually be required to cope with the difficult conditions caused by the overhanging vegetation and steep rocky banks. A 10ft salmon fly rod, or even the 8½ft sea-trout rod, could be used to fish the fly in these conditions, as the salmon are not usually big ones. A fourteen-pounder could be rated an extremely good fish in most streams.

The fly is best fished upstream and worked swiftly over the rapids; but fished deeper and more slowly in the pools. In the fastest and most rocky swims it cannot be allowed to rest long on the water, but must be constantly retrieved and re-cast. The 'take' of the salmon—if it comes—will be quick and violent. A strong arm, and strong line, and ice-cool control will be needed to hold it and to steer it away from the many obstacles that can ensnare the line. In some swims there will be many submerged rocks; unseen crevices cut into the solid rocks by countless floods. Into these the salmon will quickly plunge unless it is checked. It must be played with strength and with cunning, and must never be allowed to get far downstream. Current and rod will then tire it slowly but surely until it can be brought to the net.

Spinning

Spinning with a large copper or silver spoon involves less risk of getting tangled up in the thick overhangs of bushes and, for salmon, need not differ from the spinning methods already described for brown trout and sea-trout. A fast retrieve is essential in the shallow water, while the deeper pools can be spun over more slowly, and much deeper. Strong tackle is essential, otherwise the salmon will be lost when it hits the spoon. A spinning rod, 8–9ft long, and a fixed-spool reel loaded with 8lb breaking-strain line, is recommended.

While the water is coloured, spinning is a favourite method and one which will certainly catch some salmon; but if you disapprove of it then consider the upstream worm. This calls for greater skill, is far less likely to injure the salmon, and can be a deadly method even when the water is low. It is more effective when there is some colour in the water, but there is no need to restrict its use to this period.

Worming

Certain methods of fishing the worm are traditionally associated with salmon, but most of them have little application to fishing narrow, rocky, overgrown streams. True, there are a few pools in which it is possible to leger a bunch of worms, but this is a rather boring, static method that needs patience rather than skill. Far better to keep on the move and meet the varying challenges of the many different swims encountered as one progresses upstream. The 10ft carp rod is an excellent rod to use for this style of fishing.

Some swims are so overgrown as to give the impression of a tunnel beneath which the water flows dark and glassy. In other places the water gushes between tall, serrated slabs of rock, or flows in a long gushing curve against a steep bank. Each swim must be studied carefully and approached with caution. The worm is then flicked upstream and allowed to fall back slowly in the current. While this is happening the rod should never be pointed at the bait, but held up at an angle across the stream. The bite when it comes will take the form of a sudden surge upstream, or an unmistakable tightening of the line. Or it may be signalled by a slight cessation in the downstream movement of the line. It could be that the worm has caught round a rock or some other obstruction, but the check may also have been caused by a salmon, lying deep and almost stationary against the soft sand of the river bed, or tucked up close against the sheer sides of the rocks. Tighten carefully. Await the faint tremor that signals a taking fish. Then strike.

The experience of hooking a salmon in a swim of this nature is almost indescribable. At first, one is exhilarated and excited, but the mood soon passes as the salmon begins to fight and is replaced by a dull fear that it may escape. And it is at this stage that the battle is usually won or lost. The salmon is strong and in its natural element; but as long as it is kept within the limits of the swim its fighting power is diminished. Everything the angler does must therefore be aimed at containing it. It must not be held on a tight line or it may break free. Yet nor must the line be allowed to fall slack, or the hook may lose its hold. The salmon must be held firmly, but at the same time permitted some movement so that it is constantly forging upstream against the current and against the tension of rod and line. This it will almost always do, provided the angler remains downstream of it. Time, and the constant pressure of rod and current, will inevitably tire it, and only then can it safely be brought to the net.

Afterwards you may wonder how such a big fish could have lain concealed in such a tiny pool, and by what combination of luck, skill, and chance you managed to find, defeat and land it. It is an experience you will never forget, and one which you will certainly long to repeat.

16

Small-Stream Care and Preservation

MAKING IT PAY

IN PRE-INDUSTRIAL days, before the evils of pollution and abstraction began to affect our waterways, innumerable small rivers and streams provided fine trout and coarse fishing. Even in the comparatively recent pre-war days, many streams were unaffected by pollution, their waters running clear and sweet over beds of sand and gravel. And most of them held fish—even the tiny, shallow streams that ran close to a motorway or through a town.

Today, alas, the picture is very different. Many such streams have fallen victim to what we call industrial 'progress', poisoned by effluents or seeping sewage. Others have been allowed to become completely overgrown, or silted up, and are no longer fishable. This is not only a loss which the countryside as a whole can ill-afford but also short-sightedness on the part of many landowners to whom a properly-managed stream could provide a useful source of additional income, as well as pleasure to many local anglers. Nowadays, every mile of fishable water is in demand from an ever increasing number of anglers, and many clubs are willing to pay high prices for the privilege of fishing in a few miles of a stream or small river.

No matter how small or insignificant a stream may appear, or how overgrown it has become, it can in many cases be made to pay its way. If it already contains fish, the landowner has only to ensure that it is kept clean and, if necessary, made fishable by the judicious cutting back of encroaching vegetation. If there are no fish in the stream, it can be stocked with either trout or coarse fish, or even with both—provided it is not polluted. This might mean additional work and some outlay of capital, but it is surely better to invest in improvements of this nature than to allow the stream to become neglected, or even worse, to have it dredged and made into a straight, featureless, ditch containing no fish at all.

DREDGING

'A great sameness greets the eye. The clean gravel scours—beloved by basking dace and chub—lie covered under inches of black, dredged mud.'

These words were used by a writer to describe a stretch of the Bedfordshire Ouse after the local river board had completed its campaign of 'improvement', and they could equally well be applied to all too many similar scenes in many parts of the British Isles.

The local river boards who are mainly responsible for carrying out these dredging operations claim that they are often necessary to allow surface water to run off more quickly and so reduce the risk of flooding. Even so, is it really necessary to dredge out the entire width of the river or stream, to remove every weed-bed, every gravelly ridge, and to reduce the stream to little more than a canal, when it would seem just as effective to remove only the worst of the mud and silt and leave most of the natural formation of the river intact?

Even the reason given for dredging—to prevent flooding—is suspect, because once the natural barriers of weed and shallows are removed the water rushes downstream much more quickly and so undermines and destroys most of the softer parts of the banks. This debris is then carried away downstream by the water and, as soon as the floods subside, is deposited on the river bed where it builds up again, necessitating further dredging operations and forming a natural haven for water-lilies, arrowheads, and other less desirable plants. The whole character of the river is thus altered and the dredging operation is, in a sense, self-defeating, since it only perpetuates the problem it was originally intended to solve.

It would seem wiser to dredge out only those areas where mud or weed have accumulated in such quantities that they impede the natural flow of the stream. The shallow, gravelly ridges, and the majority of the weed-beds, should be left intact, or reduced by having a channel cut *through* them. This would quicken the flow of the stream without destroying its essential, natural formation.

The benefits which anglers are sometimes alleged to derive from these operations—such as the removal of weeds and easier access to the water—are, in fact, small compensations for the destruction wrought by the dredger. The removal of weeds and bankside shubbery lessens rather than heightens the angler's chances, since he no longer has the advantage of the cover provided by these natural obstacles and can easily be seen by every fish lying in the clear, shallow water. Most anglers would much prefer to have the river or stream left in a more natural state, and if more river boards were to consult local angling associations before dredging operations were put in hand, many streams might not only be saved from ruination but considerably improved as angling waters.

ABSTRACTION

The demand for clean water increases every year and, inevitably many small rivers and streams have been affected in consequence. Some are but pale ghosts of what they once were; others have been literally sucked dry. Few, if any, fish remain in the pathetic trickles of water which run between the bared rocks of the shallows, and anglers are seldom to be seen on their banks. The Hertfordshire chalk streams, the Rib, Beane and Oughter, are typical examples of the effect abstraction can have on a small river: reduced flow, silting, and excessive growth of weed. It is a sad story which has many parallels in other parts of the country, too.

From the angler's point of view the worst evil of abstraction is that it lowers the water table, sometimes so drastically—as in the case of the river Garry in Perthshire—that the river virtually ceases to exist. Shallows which were once covered by several inches of water often become mere trickles, running slowly between bleached stones. Along both banks broad expanses of sand and gravel are left bare and dry. In the deeper, slower-moving stretches weeds flourish, and within a few years, or months even, abstraction can alter the whole character of a river.

Abstraction also affects the fish life. Lovers of swift-running water, the trout and the grayling, may disappear completely and be replaced by coarse fish such as pike, roach, and bream. During long periods of drought all fish will be affected by the extremely low water, especially in the mud-bottomed pools where there is a heavy growth of weed. The heat starts a process of decomposition in the mud, and the oxygen content of the water is dangerously reduced. In many cases the fish will be forced to fall back gradually downstream, eventually to enter the main river, or a lake, where the environment is more favourable. Thus, in a comparatively short space of time abstraction can turn what was once a healthy stream containing many different species of fish into a mere trickle containing little else but minnows and sticklebacks.

Obviously, demands for water must be met, but no stream or river should be subjected to abstraction on such a scale that it is virtually destroyed; and to abstract water from a stream at its source is equivalent to cutting off its life flow. Water from a stream should be taken from a point as far downstream as is feasible, and whenever possible, should later be returned, after purification, to the same stream.

It is an odd reflection on our 'technological age' that while our need for new reserves of fresh water becomes increasingly more urgent, at times of flood we allow many millions of gallons of it to rush unchecked and unstored down to the sea bringing ever nearer the day when England will become a land of dried-up watercourses.

POLLUTION

Pollution has been responsible for the demise of many streams and can take several forms: the discharge of untreated sewage or industrial wastes; the run-off of acids or tars from roadways or mine-workings; or from chemical sprays used on neighbouring farmlands to kill weeds or unwanted insects. Streams are particularly susceptible to pollution from farms, and in 1966 twenty cases of pollution resulting from the discharge of wastes from pea factories were reported in Lincolnshire alone. In Wales, an overflow of silage from nearby pits caused the death of more than 1,000 trout in the river Ythan, while waste from a sugar-beet factory created a barrier of deoxygenated water that swept down the river Eden, killing all fish on its way downstream. More recently, in July 1972, a four mile stretch of one of the best coarse-fishing rivers in England, the Suffolk Stow, was so polluted with barbasca, a compound of derris used in insecticides, that fish died in their thousands, swans and ducks had to be moved downstream and farmers were warned not to graze cattle on water meadows.

Chemical pollution is perhaps the most disastrous of all forms, and certainly the most immediate in its effect. A discharge of naphthalene into the river Ouse in Buckinghamshire killed thousands of fish, and the accidental release of ammonia into the river Brue in Somerset, caused by a fracture in the cooling system of a dairy, caused similar large-scale fatalities amongst the fish population.

The most disastrous fish kill from this source occurred in America in 1963 when approximately 5 million fish in the river Mississippi died as a result of pollution from eldrin—a chemical used as spray to combat insect pests in nearby sugar-cane fields. Fish in the streams that ran through the fields died at once; those in the main river died more slowly, and much intense investigation was needed before the source of pollution was finally traced.

The most disturbing aspect of pollution by hydro-carbon-based pesticides is the way in which the chemical is built up, not only in the tissues of fish but also in the bodies of animals and birds that prey upon the fish. Research workers in Canada discovered that when DDT was sprayed upon the surrounding forests in June, young salmon were found dead in the stream the following autumn. The DDT had been stored in their tissues until the falling temperature caused the fish to call upon their reserves of fat, and was then distributed throughout their vital organs, so causing their death.

Another investigation, undertaken by research workers in California, revealed that microscopic organisms in a selected environment contained only five parts per million of DDT; yet the fish contained 2,000 parts per million, due to ingestion of large quantities of these organisms. The build-up continues throughout the chain, with birds, animals, and sometimes human beings as well, being the final consumers and recipients of the chemical.

In a country as congested as Britain, and with the demand for clean water increasing yearly, enforcement of the strictest possible measures to prevent further pollution of rivers and streams becomes of vital importance. Exhaustive tests should be carried out by independent bodies on all new insecticides, and a stricter control exercised over their use. Too little is yet known about the effect of water-borne chemical pollutants on the human system for anyone to be complacent.

Signs of Pollution

Some signs of pollution are easy to detect. Fish mortality, or evidence of sickness, is one obvious sign, but by then it is often too late for remedial measures to be effective. An earlier sign of an unhealthy water is likely to be the absence, or dying-off, of certain kinds of weed. Starwort is sometimes killed by organic pollution, and pondweed is susceptible to a high degree of detergent pollution. Indeed, most weeds in an affected stream will show signs of unhealthy growth, and will *look* sick.

An abundance of certain forms of animal life, or a decrease in the numbers of others, provides another clue to the presence of pollution. Animals which thrive in clean, well-oxygenated water, such as shrimps and various kinds of nymphs, rapidly move away from or die in polluted water, and are eventually replaced by the freshwater louse and leeches, both of which are commonly found in polluted waters.

When the pollution is persistent there may be a complete absence of weeds and animal life. The bottom of the stream is often covered with fungus or mud, which has a characteristic sulphurous odour when disturbed. Sticklebacks are usually the first fish to reappear after pollution, and their presence could indicate an improvement. Minnows, bullheads, and gudgeon are also found in some semi-polluted waters, but the larger coarse fish, though more resistant to pollution than trout, are usually to be found only in streams and rivers that are not permanently polluted.

Any sign of pollution should be reported immediately to the local river board and, if possible, samples of the water taken immediately to enable analysts to establish the cause of pollution, and to try to trace it to its source. Proceedings may then be taken against the offender with a view to preventing further pollution and, possibly, claiming compensation for any loss of fish. Farmers who carelessly allow organic farmyard waste, or chemicals used for crop spraying, to seep into nearby streams remain the most difficult pollutors to trace. Others have realised that much of this waste has a high value as a fertiliser, and are now spraying it back onto the land to the benefit of themselves and the angler. It is to be hoped that this practice will become more common.

MAINTENANCE

A healthy stream usually contains a wide variety of different swims, has a luxuriant growth of weed, and is usually well stocked with several different species of fish. If all seems well, it is a wise policy to leave the stream as it is. Interference with the existing ecology of the water, however well intentioned, may have disastrous effects later. It is all too easy to take a step in the wrong direction, but much more difficult to retrace that step once any serious damage has been done.

The first essential is to check on the purity of the water as it is useless to contemplate any further steps until any pollution that may exist has been identified and eradicated. A water recovering from recent pollution would probably contain little if any plant-life and would need to be replanted first with suitable weeds. In the normal course of events, weeds would gradually re-establish themselves as the amount of pollution in the water decreased, but the process can be speeded up by the planting of selected weeds. In his book, *The Management of Coarse Fishing Waters*, Eric Birch suggests water-buttercups, water-celery, and mare's tail, for the swift-moving water, and starwort, curly pondweed and milfoil for the deeper, slower-moving stretches.

Some anglers seem to have a strong aversion to weeds, but they are essential to both fish and animal life; and a water that is deficient in both does not often produce good fish—as witness the stunted trout of the barren mountain streams. Some cutting back of weeds is sometimes desirable, or even essential when they have grown to such an extent that they block the free passage of water. When this happens *some* of the weeds should be removed, preferably from the centre of the stream where the flow of water is usually most brisk.

Plants that are removed should be dug up rather than just cut off as, if the roots are left in, the plants will reappear the following year. No cutting or removal should be attempted in the spring as plants then provide essential shelter for the hordes of newly-hatched fry, and all such work is best left until the autumn when the fry will have had a chance to establish themselves.

From the angler's point of view it is also desirable to have a healthy bankside growth of reeds, such as the sedges, reed-mace, or yellow iris, together with bushes and small trees, such as willow, alder, or hawthorn. These all serve to provide cover for the angler, and too drastic pruning, far less wholesale removal, is very much to be discouraged. Most trees which have been heavily pruned or lopped take many years to grow again, and may never recover. Willows recover more rapidly than most and are one of the best trees to plant along the banks of a stream.

Only when the bankside growth is so dense that it virtually shuts out all light from the water should it be cut back, and then only to a limited extent. There is no more depressing sight than rows and rows of tree stumps where there was once a line of beautiful trees. Remove a few at intervals. Trim back some of the overhanging branches to let in more light. But leave the rest. Both angler and the fish will have cause to appreciate the cover they provide.

Mud is another thing that some anglers abhor and advocate removing, but a little mud will not harm either angler or fish, and provides a valuable breeding-ground for the gnats and midges upon whose larvae the fry of most species, and also many adult fish, often feed. Only if the mud threatens to choke up the stream or becomes a prolific breeding-ground for unwanted plants should it be removed. In the normal course of events weed clearance is all that is necessary, when the increased flow of the current will carry away any excess mud.

STOCKING

Acquiring a fishery of one's own can be an exciting experience and the angler's first impulse will probably be to try to improve the water. He wants, above all, to make the fishing better—by which he usually means that he wants to be able to catch more fish more easily. If the fish are not easy to catch or his initial catches do not live up to his expectations, he is apt to presume—quite often mistakenly—that there are not enough fish in the water. The quickest and easiest solution seems to be to put more in.

Before doing this he should first ask himself if his own tactics are not at fault. Quite often fish in those streams that are plentifully endowed with food are not easy to catch because they are surrounded by an abundance of food and do not need the angler's baits. In contrast, fish in streams where natural food is in short supply will be eagerly looking for it, and will therefore be comparatively easy to catch. Thus, streams containing a plentiful supply of natural foods will sometimes appear to be understocked, while those that are deficient in this respect will appear to be quite normal and healthy.

If the angler reaches such a conclusion he may be very wrong. Waters in which the fish are difficult to catch are often well-stocked with good fish, and may contain fish of specimen size. On the other hand, waters in which the fish are relatively easy to catch will probably be overstocked with certain species, and it would be most unwise to add to their numbers until more is known about the stocks the water already holds.

Prolonged and determined fishing will often reveal a different picture from that which the angler had originally formed. A water which at first appeared to contain few fish will often produce many fine fish of several different species. If so, the wisest policy would be to refrain from any interference with the existing stocks.

A period spent examining the water while it is running low and clear will also prove informative, as it is then often possible to actually see the fish and so gain a rough idea as to the numbers and size of each species that the stream holds. A pair of Polaroid spectacles is invaluable for this purpose, especially if there is any sun on the water.

Another, and perhaps more conclusive step is to employ a fishery consultant to make a thorough examination of the stream and its fish population, either by netting or by electro-fishing. It will then be possible not only to determine how many of each different species of fish live in the stream, but also to assess their rate of growth. Such a survey might reveal a well-balanced fish population with a healthy and normal rate of growth; if so, it would be unwise to put in more fish. On the other hand, it might reveal an over-abundance of certain species, with consequent poor growth rates. Some streams contain hordes of stunted roach, rudd, or perch, many of which could be removed in order to reduce the competition for available food. In particular, it would be beneficial to reduce the numbers of fish that compete for the same kinds of foods, such as roach, rudd, dace, and bream. No stream could possibly support an over-abundance of all these species.

Obviously, any water can only produce good fish when the number in it does not exceed the available food supply, and there are two ways of improving a water which is over-populated with fish. One is to increase the supply of natural foods by encouraging weed-growth and animal life; the other is to reduce drastically the numbers of fish in that water. To adopt any other course is to risk upsetting the whole delicate balance of life in the water, and if in any doubt it is best to do nothing.

Predators

The part predators, such as pike, perch, and trout, play in the overall ecology of any water is often the cause of controversy. Some claim that predators are essential to keep down the stocks of other fish. Yet there are waters in which there are no pike or perch, and yet plenty of big chub, roach, or rudd. On the other hand, waters which hold both pike and perch may contain only *small* fish of other species. Obviously then, factors other than the presence or absence of predators affect the growth and numbers of other fish in the water. Everything considered, if the water already contains big fish of other species it would be unwise to introduce any predators; but if the water is overpopulated with rudd or roach then the introduction of a few pike or perch could be considered as an alternative method of reducing the numbers of other fish. The quickest and most effective method, though, is to remove large numbers of *small* fish, leaving the remainder, which have already attained a fair size, to grow bigger. Once predators are established in a water they soon multiply, and it is difficult to remove them. Their introduction is not, therefore, a step that should lightly be taken.

TROUT FISHERIES

Some anglers prefer to have a stream stocked with trout only, and so pursue a policy of eliminating coarse fish altogether. The only justification for this policy would seem to be that it does create a fishery in which only trout will be caught, but any idea that trout cannot live happily with coarse fish, and grow to a large size, is completely false. There are many streams in which trout live in company with several different species of coarse fish, and often these streams produce trout of specimen size. In streams where the trout are consistently small, their poor growth rate can usually be traced back to a basic deficiency in the water itself, rather than to the presence of other fish. A healthy stream can normally support both coarse fish and trout, and the trout may, in fact, be healthier, and gamer fighters, because of the competition from other fish.

However, if it is decided that the fishery should be given over wholly to trout, the coarse fish should be removed, either by electro-fishing or by netting, and then transferred to other waters, where they may be welcomed. The stream can then be stocked with young trout, which should be given time to get acclimatised to their new environment. The practice of stocking a water with large adult trout is to be deplored. Hatchery-bred trout are usually so ridiculously easy to catch, that it certainly cannot be called angling.

Certain types of streams are, obviously, more suitable for trout than others and, a typical lowland stream containing a large head of coarse fish would not come into this category, since it would be practically impossible to eradicate the coarse fish entirely. The smaller, faster-flowing stream—or even the mountain stream—is much more suitable, provided there are sufficient holding pools to allow essential weed-growth. In this type of stream, where coarse fish are usually present only in limited numbers or may be absent altogether, there should be excellent prospects of establishing and maintaining a flourishing trout fishery.

Index